3 1994 01391 3840

9/08

SANTA

D0399075

THE TRUTH ABOUT

AVOIDING SCAMS

364.163 WEI
Weisman, Steve
The truth about avoiding
   scams

                         $18.99
CENTRAL   31994013913840

Steve Weisman

© 2008 by Pearson Education, Inc.

Publishing as FT Press

Upper Saddle River, New Jersey 07458

FT Press offers excellent discounts on this book when ordered in quantity for bulk purchases or special sales. For more information, please contact U.S. Corporate and Government Sales, 1-800-382-3419, corpsales@pearsontechgroup.com. For sales outside the U.S., please contact International Sales at international@pearsoned.com.

Company and product names mentioned herein are the trademarks or registered trademarks of their respective owners.

All rights reserved. No part of this book may be reproduced, in any form or by any means, without permission in writing from the publisher.

Printed in the United States of America

First Printing January 2008

ISBN-10:   0-13-233385-6

ISBN-13: 978-0-13-233385-6

Pearson Education LTD.
Pearson Education Australia PTY, Limited.
Pearson Education Singapore, Pte. Ltd.
Pearson Education North Asia, Ltd.
Pearson Education Canada, Ltd.
Pearson Educatión de Mexico, S.A. de C.V.
Pearson Education—Japan
Pearson Education Malaysia, Pte. Ltd.

Vice President, Publisher
Tim Moore

Associate Publisher and Director of Marketing
Amy Neidlinger

Executive Editor
Jim Boyd

Editorial Assistant
Pamela Boland

Development Editor
Russ Hall

Digital Marketing Manager
Julie Phifer

Marketing Coordinator
Megan Colvin

Cover and Interior Designs
Stuart Jackman,
Dorling Kindersley

Managing Editor
Gina Kanouse

Senior Project Editor
Lori Lyons

Copy Editor
Karen Gill

Design Manager
Sandra Schroeder

Senior Compositor
Gloria Schurick

Proofreader
San Dee Phillips

Manufacturing Buyer
Dan Uhrig

Library of Congress Cataloging-in-Publication Data

Weisman, Steve.
  The truth about avoiding scams / Steve Weisman.
     p. cm.
  ISBN 0-13-233385-6 (pbk. : alk. paper) 1. Swindlers and swindling. 2. Fraud. 3. Computer crimes. I. Title.
  HV6691.W43 2008
  364.16'3--dc22

                             2007029594

This book is dedicated to two very important women in my life:

to Fran Borek, whose never wavering support and faith in me
makes me strive to be as good as she thinks I am;

and to my wife Carole, my partner in life, who makes me smile.

Scams and fraud have been a part of history since the dawn of time. Many of the new scams we see today are not new at all but just variations on old cons. Schemes around in the 1500s and referred to as the Spanish Prisoner Scam have morphed over time to become the Nigerian Letter Scam of today. Claims of medical charlatans were as attractive to the early American colonists as they are to us now.

Clever con artists can manipulate every human need and desire. After all, they are the only criminals known as artists. And as much as we rightfully deplore their actions, we must recognize their art to better defend ourselves. Scam artists adapt their art to paint whatever picture they sense will make us vulnerable to their con. They know how to appeal to our own particular weaknesses and psychological makeup. They appeal to whatever works. They construct a network of "people like us" whom we trust; they trumpet legitimate and impressive-sounding business connections; they appeal to our fears; they appeal to our friendship; they appeal to our optimism; they appeal to our desire for quick and easy solutions to life's problems; and they appeal to our greed. Sometimes they even appeal to and exploit that little kernel of dishonesty that many people have.

According to the Federal Trade Commission, every year more than ten percent of Americans lose more than a billion dollars to scams. Interestingly, the largest group of victims is between the ages of 25 and 44; ages when you are young enough to know everything—which, of course, makes you more vulnerable to a scammer. Particularly troublesome is a study by the National Association of Securities Dealers which indicates that wealthy people, who are financially literate and astute, are actually more likely to be suckered in by a financial scam. The only defense against scammers is knowledge and skepticism. This book provides you with some of both. It teaches you how to recognize and avoid scams.

Being aware of the criminals who are out to take your money is not enough. A scam by any other name is still a scam, and unfortunately, there are some scams that are perfectly legal that can cause you to lose money. Or perhaps they are imperfectly legal, but at this point in time, the law may not be on your side. A good example of a legal scam is what credit card companies can do legally in many instances.

So read this book and gain the knowledge that can protect your wallet. This book teaches you the truth about scams and how to keep from becoming a victim of both illegal and legal scams.

TRUTH

Identity theft—your money or your life

ou may fool all the people some of the time, you can even fool some of the people all of the time, but you cannot fool all of the people all of the time.

—*Abraham Lincoln*

ut you can come awfully close if people aren't careful.

—*Steve Weisman*

"We're number one." That chant can be heard at many sporting events. Being number one generally is a position of great prominence. However, when it comes to scams, being number one is a dubious distinction. Identity theft is and will be for the foreseeable future number one among scams. More than a third of all fraud complaints to the Federal Trade Commission are for identity theft. In 2006, 14 million Americans were victims of identity theft.

Identity theft occurs when someone obtains your personal information, such as a credit card number or a Social Security number, and then either uses this information to gain access to your accounts or uses it to obtain credit in your name and run up enormous bills that come back as black marks on your credit report.

> More than a third of all fraud complaints to the Federal Trade Commission are for identity theft.

Identity theft is an attractive growth industry in the criminal world. It is easy to accomplish and difficult to catch. It can be done through high tech, low tech, or no tech. Identity thieves obtain your personal information by sophisticated computer tactics that trick you into providing your personal information, or they can obtain it by going through your garbage for credit card applications that you have thrown in the trash. You may be victimized by organized criminals continents away or by members of your own family. Identity theft is everywhere.

The damage to your credit report is one of the most harmful aspects of identity theft. The information contained in your credit report is used by the credit reporting agencies to calculate your credit score. The range of credit scores is between 300 and 850. The higher your score, the better your credit. Your ability to get a car loan, credit card, or a mortgage loan as well as the interest rate for which you will be eligible is affected by your credit score. Many people are unaware that their credit score affects the interest rate that they will be offered on loans or credit cards. Your ability to get a job, obtain insurance, or rent an apartment is often dependent upon your credit score. When you are the victim of identity theft, the misuse of your credit by the identity thief can drastically reduce your credit score, thereby making your life much more difficult and expensive. It is a complicated, frustrating, and time-consuming task to try to correct your credit report after you have been the victim of identity theft. Identity theft can be like herpes: You have it for life. Once you have been victimized, it can come back to haunt you, even years later.

One of the latest identity theft twists is medical identity theft, or the theft of a person's identity to access his health insurance. The effects on the victim can be enormous. In addition to the usual damage to your credit for unpaid bills, your medical treatment could be based on the identity thief's medical history. You could receive a prescription that harmfully interacts with other prescriptions you take. You could even receive a blood transfusion of the wrong blood type. Credit records can be difficult to correct following an identity theft, but medical records can be almost impossible to fix due to medical privacy laws.

Medical identity theft is often an inside job. An employee of the health care provider gives the information to identity thieves, who in turn sell the information to people needing medical care. Sometimes, however, medical identity theft is an outside job, where the identity thieves go through the trash of a health care provider.

> Medical records can be almost impossible to fix due to medical privacy laws.

Protect yourself from medical identity theft as you would from any identity theft by shredding medical bills and records that you are discarding. In addition, keep an updated copy of your medical records that your physician maintains. Always read any communications from your health insurance provider carefully, regardless of how difficult they sometimes are to understand. Ask your health insurance provider to give you a list of all payments made in your name. If you find any irregularities, you can follow up with both your physician and the credit reporting bureaus.

TRUTH

2

Go phish

Conmen construct counterfeit websites that appear to be those of legitimate companies but, in fact, are just a way of hooking you into providing personal information that can be mined for identity theft. This scam is called phishing.

Phishing occurs when an identity thief lures you through a phony email that purports to be from a bank or other legitimate company to a bogus website that looks like the website of the legitimate company that the scammers pretend to be. This website requires you to provide personal financial information to verify your account or even allegedly to protect you from the very type of fraud that you are about to become a victim of. One telltale flaw in phishing schemes is that although the website to which you link from the phony email appears to be legitimate, if you look closely at the web address, you will notice that it is not correct. Unfortunately, many victims do not notice that the domain name does not match the site to which they have been directed.

One early phishing expedition set up a phony America Online website. The conmen sent email messages to their victims claiming that there was a problem with their America Online accounts and, if they did not update their billing information, their AOL accounts would be canceled, causing a loss of Internet access. The email message directed the victims to click on a hyperlink contained in the fraudulent email to reach the AOL Billing Center. The people who did this ended up at a website that looked amazingly like the real AOL website, but it was a phony. The unwary victims were then instructed to provide the credit card numbers for the cards they used to pay their AOL accounts. They were also asked for a new credit card number to replace the one that was alleged to have resulted in the original problem with the billing. In one variation of this con, the scammer also asked for the customer's name, mother's maiden

One telltale flaw in phishing schemes is that although the website to which you link from the phony email appears to be legitimate, if you look closely at the web address, you will notice that it is not correct.

name, billing address, Social Security number, bank routing number, and AOL screen names and passwords, a veritable mother load of potential identity theft information.

Another phishing expedition involves an email from your bank with information to help you avoid identity theft. It tells you that the bank can provide you with a special security system that will generate online codes with which you can conduct online business without the fear that your personal information will be compromised. The email goes on to tell you that all you need to do to register for this service is to click on the link contained in the email to direct you to the website to register for the security system. That is the carrot approach. However, the same email also uses the stick approach and informs you that if you do not complete the application for the new security system, your online access to your bank account will be temporarily suspended for security reasons.

The email looks quite authentic. I received such an email and might have even been tempted to respond to it had I actually been an account holder at the national bank that contacted me about my account. Scammers send out waves of emails without knowing who is and who is not a customer of the particular bank. It's a numbers game to them that at least some of the people who get the emails will indeed be customers of the bank and fall for the scam.

If you click on to the link to which the email directs you, you are also in danger of unwittingly downloading a Trojan horse keystroke-logging program without your being aware of it that can provide the scammer with passwords and other important information from your computer that can be used to defraud you. Even worse, if you go to the website to which you are directed, you will find that you are asked, for identification purposes, to provide your user ID and password, which in turn gives the scammers all the information they need to empty your account at that bank.

TIP You can install many kinds of antiphishing software on your computer that will warn you if you are on a known phishing site. A good one that is available free is Netcraft, which you can download at www.toolbar.netcraft.com.

The truth is, *your bank or Internet server will never contact you in this manner.* If you get an email that purports to be a notice that an account of yours will be closed unless you reconfirm your billing information, *do not* follow the prompts to reply or click on any hyperlinks contained in the email. Instead, contact the real company at a telephone number that you already know to be accurate and inquire about your account.

TRUTH

Vishing down on the pharm

First came phishing; then came pharming and vishing. Perhaps next will come spelling lessons. Pharming and vishing are next steps in the evolution of phishing.

Pharming involves a virus or malicious program, sometimes called malware, that is secretly installed on your computer, often through an attachment to an apparently innocuous email or attached to music or other free downloads from sites with which you may not be familiar. And that is one of the key lessons. Never download from sites with which you are not totally familiar. Just as you would instruct your children not to take candy from strangers, you should also instruct them never to download music, games, or anything else from an unknown source. There is just too much of a risk of malware. Once the malware is installed on your computer, you may, in the course of your normal computer use, correctly type in the name of a bank or other company with which you do business but end up being directed to a phony website even though the domain name that appears on the address line may indicate the correct, legitimate address of the bank or other business you were trying to contact. The truth is that the address of the legitimate website has been hijacked by the identity thieves, and their malware is now imbedded in your computer. Once you arrive at the phony website, if you succumb to the requests for personal information on the website, you are on your way to becoming a victim of identity theft.

The truth is, you should never click on links within emails from people with whom you're not familiar. Don't provide personal information online to anyone with whom you are not totally familiar. And, of course, keep your computer as secure as possible through the use of spam filters and antivirus and antispyware software along with a good firewall. It is also critical to keep that protective software current because scammers are constantly improving their technology.

> Never download music, games, or anything else from an unknown source. There is just too much of a risk of malware.

Vishing takes advantage of a new technological advance for a scam. Voice over Internet Protocol (VoIP) is a new technology that permits people to make telephone calls through their computer instead of a phone line. If you call a regular telephone number from your computer, your voice converts into a digital signal that transmits over the Internet and then converts to a regular telephone signal when it reaches the regular telephone that you want to call.

People who would be wary of an email message purporting to be from their bank or credit card company telling them that their security has been breached are more likely to trust a message they receive in a telephone call. And that is just what the scammers do in a new technique that is known as vishing. A recorded phone message is sent out by computers using Voice over Internet Protocol technology to vast numbers of potential victims telling them that their bank account or credit card security has been breached and that they should call the security office of the bank or credit card company immediately. Once the victim calls the number, a prerecorded message tells them that for account verification, they need to provide their name as well as their bank account number or credit card number. When they provide this information, their security actually is breached because this is a scam.

The truth is, if you were to receive such a legitimate call regarding your bank account or credit card, it would not be through a prerecorded message. In addition, you should never call the number provided to you by an unsolicited telephone call. Instead, you should go to your monthly bank statement or credit card statement and retrieve the telephone number for your bank or credit card company that you know is legitimate. You can then call the company to see if the call to you was legitimate.

> **You should never call the number provided to you by an unsolicited telephone call.**

TRUTH

4

Do Not Call Registry, Patriot Act scams

Many scams come about through telemarketing. Although legitimate companies use telemarketing, the combination of annoyance that many people feel when they receive telemarketing calls coupled with the increased risk of fraud in a telemarketing call where you receive information that is impossible to verify while you are speaking with the telemarketer makes many people choose to enroll in the Do Not Call list established by the federal government. Enroll by going online to www.donotcall.gov or by calling 888-382-1222.

The national Do Not Call Registry set up by Congress permits you to enroll as part of a list of people who telemarketers are prohibited from calling. It works. However, anything can be turned into another opportunity for scammers. Although it may seem somewhat ironic, scammers have called people on the telephone telling them that they are with the Do Not Call list and they need information to sign them up. They then use this information to make you a victim of identity theft. Don't fall for this ploy. The real Do Not Call Registry does not call.

Whatever is in the news can be turned into a scam by clever scammers—from natural disasters such as Hurricane Katrina, to antiterrorist legislation such as the Patriot Act. Many people have received emails purporting to be from the Federal Deposit Insurance Corporation, or FDIC. The email looks legitimate. It's not. The FDIC will never contact you by email. The email you receive from the conman tells you that the Director of Homeland Security is suspending all deposit insurance on your bank accounts due to possible violations of the Patriot Act. The email goes on to urge you to provide personal identifying information to revive your FDIC insurance, which you can do by clicking on the link in the email. The website you are linked to in the email, which purports to be an FDIC website, is a phishing expedition run by some not very patriotic conmen. You will be asked to provide personal information, including your Social Security number. Once the scammer obtains this information, he uses it to make you a victim of identity theft. You should ignore any emails you receive that say they are from the FDIC. If you are concerned that there may be a real problem with your bank accounts, call the FDIC at a telephone number you know to be accurate.

TRUTH

Protect yourself from identity theft

Follow these guidelines to protect yourself from identity theft:

1. Don't give out your personal information on the phone to someone you have not called.

2. Don't give your personal information online to anyone you have not contacted directly, and be sure that the company with which you are dealing is legitimate.

3. Check your credit report annually. It's free. Go to https://www. annualcreditreport.com/cra/index.jsp or call 877-322-8228.

4. Don't carry your Social Security card in your wallet.

5. Don't use your Social Security number for identification purposes unless you're required to do so by law. Generally, you are not required to provide your Social Security number to a business unless the company is required to report transactions to the Internal Revenue Service. Unfortunately, many businesses ask for your Social Security number for their own identification purposes, and there are few laws to prevent them from doing so. If a company asks for your Social Security number, don't give it immediately. Ask the company to use an alternate number such as your driver's license number. The Government Accountability Office (www.gao.gov) has compiled a list of state laws that limit the use of Social Security numbers. You can consult this list to learn about the rights you have in your particular home state.

6. It has been against the law since December 17, 2005, for states to use your Social Security number as your driver's license number, but many people still have older driver's licenses that are not yet up for renewal that display their Social Security number. Ask for a new license without your Social Security number.

7. Take yourself off the list to receive those nuisance preapproved credit card offers. Identity thieves retrieve these from the trash and apply for credit cards in your name. Call 888-5-OPT-OUT or go online to www.optoutprescreen.com to get your name removed from the lists used to generate preapproved credit card offers. You need to enter your name, phone number, address, and Social Security number. You can take yourself off the list for five years or permanently. I suggest permanently.

8. Change your health insurance card number from your Social Security number.

9. Check websites that require personal data. See if the web address bar begins with https rather than just http. The "s" means that the website is protected by SSL (Secure Sockets Layer) security that encrypts your data. Look for a closed padlock image in the bottom-right corner. Double-click on the padlock to check that the website's security certificate is genuine and up-to-date. The padlock indicates that your information is being encrypted.

10. Shred, shred, shred. Cross shredding is best, because some methamphetamine addict could stay up all night piecing together your vertically shredded trash to get information to be used to make you a victim of identity theft.

Credit freeze

You can also opt for a credit freeze. You know about the pain people experience after eating ice cream or drinking a cold beverage too quickly. (If you are academically inclined, the proper name for brain freeze is Spheno Palatine Gangleoneuralgia.) However, you may not be familiar with credit freezes, which can provide you with tremendous protection from becoming a victim of identity theft.

To evaluate an application for credit, particularly for credit to buy a large ticket item, such as expensive electronic equipment or a car, the retailer looks at your credit report to determine whether you are creditworthy. A credit freeze is a lock on your credit report that prevents your credit report from being seen by anyone unless *you* specifically, through the use of a PIN, make the credit report available. This provides a great deal of

The federal government has been reluctant to pass much-needed national credit freeze legislation, largely due to the lobbying efforts of the banking and credit industry, which would rather tolerate identity theft than do anything that would slow down impulse buying.

protection from identity theft, because even if an identity thief is able to get access to sufficient personal information of yours, such as your Social Security number, he will still not be able to access your credit report without knowing your PIN. Unfortunately, only about half of the states authorize credit freezes, and five of them permit credit freezes only after you have become a victim of identity theft. The truth is, the federal government has been reluctant to pass much-needed national credit freeze legislation, largely due to the lobbying efforts of the banking and credit industry, which would rather tolerate identity theft than do anything that would slow down impulse buying.

TRUTH

Trojan horse

"Honesty pays, but it doesn't seem to pay enough to suit some people."

—*Kin Hubbard*

Keystroke logging programs, most commonly called Trojan horses, are a kind of spyware that, once installed on your computer, monitors all activity on your computer and transmits that information back to the scammer, who uses it to access your bank accounts, credit cards, brokerage accounts, or any of your online business. This information can even be used to establish credit in your name that the scammer will use without, of course, ever paying on the account, which then turns up as a black mark on your credit report and makes your life more difficult.

The truth is, Trojan horses are aptly named because they are installed in your computer by you when you unwittingly download them. A common way they reach your computer is an infected email with an attachment that installs the program onto your computer. Sharing of songs, games, or other material through peer-to-peer usage is another way that Trojan horses are stabled in your computer. To combat this threat, you must be more than cautious when downloading anything. Certainly, don't download anything from a source you're not entirely familiar with. Even downloading attachments from friends or family is no guarantee that your computer won't be infected, because the person may unintentionally be passing the Trojan horse on to you. The best course of action is to have a good firewall and antispyware software on your computer and keep the software constantly updated.

TIP A good firewall is an essential element in protecting your computer against keystroke logging programs. But not all firewalls are created equal. Use a firewall, such as ZoneAlarm, which not only limits access to your computer, but also blocks unidentified programs on your computer from sending information back to the scammer who planted it, thereby minimizing the damage of a Trojan horse on your computer.

TRUTH

PayPal, eBay

If you have used eBay, the Internet auction site, you have probably used PayPal, which started as an independent company to help people pay for goods and services online and was bought by eBay in 2002. A phishing scam starts with an email claiming to be from PayPal telling you that it has had some computer problems and it needs you to log on to your account to confirm your personal information. However, the link takes you to a phony PayPal website. If you go there and provide the information requested, you soon become a victim of identity theft.

Another PayPal scam involves an email that purports to be from PayPal informing you that you have received money from someone. (In many instances, the name used is Betty Hill, which interestingly enough, was the name of a woman who said she was abducted by aliens in New Hampshire in 1961.) You are then directed by a link to what looks like the official PayPal site, where you are asked to input your PayPal ID and password. If you do so, your PayPal account is now in the hands of scammers. If you have any thoughts that such a letter might be real, call PayPal.

Another common PayPal scam also starts with a phony email. This one confirms your payment of hundreds of dollars for a particular item you actually have not purchased. The email also indicates that if you have not authorized the particular charge, you can click on a link to cancel the payment and receive a full refund. This takes you to an official-looking website where you are required to input personal information, including the number of any credit cards or debit cards used for your PayPal account. This is just another example of phishing used so that the scammer can get your personal information and access your accounts.

When using eBay and other online auctions, check out the references of the seller of anything you consider buying. Also, consider using an online escrow service. And never provide information to PayPal or anyone else online unless you are absolutely positive of the identity of the person. Always be skeptical when PayPal or anyone else asks for information that they should already have.

TRUTH

Second chances—eBay

Who doesn't like a second chance? Who wouldn't like a Mulligan? So when people receive an email telling them that they have another chance to bid on an item that they had lost out on because the winning eBay bidder failed to purchase the item, they are pleasantly surprised. Sometimes they are told that the winning bidder did not meet the reserve price, which is the minimum price set by the seller for sale of a particular item. What scammers do is wait until the end of an online auction and then look at the list of bidders and compose an email to losing bidders posing as the seller.

The phony email looks legitimate. However, it asks for personal information to process the bid and receive an invoice from eBay. Unfortunately, once the victim provides his or her personal information, the invoice never comes. It is a scam that provides identity thieves important information about you. Another variation of this scam involves your being permitted to rebid on an item and then being instructed to send in your winning bid by a wire transfer. Once you send in your money by wire, the money is gone, but the item never comes.

The truth is, although second chances do sometimes come in life and even in eBay, they do not come through emails directly from the seller of the item, but rather from eBay itself. Sometimes the authentic second chance offer will come in an email from eBay with a "buy it now" icon you can click on to accept the offer. The email will also provide you with a new number and page for the item.

Legitimate second chance offers also may appear as a link on the page of the particular listing. Below the message "You were outbid" will appear any second chance opportunities. Second chance offers will also appear on your "Items I Didn't Win" page on eBay.

The truth is, you should never consider emails for second chance offers that purport to be from the seller personally rather than from eBay. Never pay by a wire transfer, such as from Western Union or by a bank electronic transfer. If there is a problem with the item, you have no recourse to get your money back if you have wired it. Finally, ignore messages that do not come to your eBay email account but rather turn up in your regular email.

TRUTH

Free adult entertainment

Pornography abounds on the Internet. Fully aware of the public's apparent never-ending appetite for online adult entertainment, enterprising scammers have used this to scam people out of money through their phone bills.

A number of websites, such as the now shut-down sexygirls.com, were used in one particular scam to lure people by providing free Internet pornography that could be accessed only after downloading what was referred to as a special "viewer" program. However, what the downloaded program actually did was disconnect the computer users from their local Internet service providers and reconnect the computers to a phone number in Moldova, an Eastern European country found between Romania and the Ukraine. Consequently, when the unwary computer user went to the adult entertainment websites promoted by the scammers, he incurred international telephone charges of more than $2 per minute. To make matters worse, the program did not disconnect the computer user from the international call until the computer was turned off. Thus, even after the computer user left the particular adult entertainment website to do other online surfing, or even when the computer user was not on the Internet but merely using his computer for other purposes, such as word processing, the international call and the commensurate charges continued to accumulate so long as the computer was not turned off. The special "viewer" program also automatically turned off the computer user's modem speakers so that the computer user would not hear the disconnect or the dialing of the international number.

The lesson here is one not restricted to these particular pornographic websites. Do not download anything from a website you're not familiar with and not confident as to its legitimacy. In some instances, downloaded material may even contain Trojan horse, keystroke logging programs that can follow all your online activities and steal your passwords and personal information used online. This information, in turn, can be used to make you an identity theft victim.

> Do not download anything from a website you're not familiar with and not confident as to its legitimacy.

TRUTH

10

Two more for the road

If you can't trust Oprah

Oprah Winfrey is one of the most popular and trustworthy people in America today. So, if you got an email from Oprah, certainly you could believe that what she said was the truth—and the information contained within that email probably would be information you could rely on.

Unfortunately, for the many people who received an emailed invitation from Oprah to attend a taping of her show, the email they received was not from Oprah but from an identity thief. By the way, Oprah herself has been a victim of identity theft. It can happen to anyone. In the unsolicited email purporting to be from Oprah, the recipients were told that they would receive tickets to her show after they either verified financial information or wired money to a supplied address. As with all television shows, the *Oprah Winfrey Show* does not sell tickets. They are free. And there would be no reason for Oprah to have anyone's financial information. As always, the cardinal rule is: Never give your financial information to someone whom you have not contacted directly and whom you have not checked out for legitimacy.

From Russia, but not with love—the hit man scam

Imagine how you would feel if you opened an email and found that it was a communication from a hit man saying that he has been hired to kill you by a "friend" of yours. Apparently, the hit man remembers the quote of Eddie Cantor, "He hasn't an enemy in the world—but all his friends hate him." Fortunately, however, the hit man goes on to tell you that after following you for some time, he has decided that if you pay him a sum, typically ranging from $80,000 to $150,000, he will let you live. The FBI has tracked a number of these emails to Russia. They are a total scam. There is no hit man. The goal of the people behind this particular scam is to either get you to part with your money or induce you to provide them with personal information that can be used for identity theft. Either way, you lose. If you receive such an email, many of which have come from 1wayout@myway.com, report it to the FBI and the Internet Crime Complaint Center (IC3) at www.ic3.gov.

TRUTH

Ponzi scheme

he sure way to be cheated is to think one's self more cunning than others.

—*Francois De La Rochefoucauld*

If scammers had a national holiday, it would be March 3—it was on March 3, 1882, that Charles Ponzi was born. Ponzi was the early scammer who conned Bostonians through a scam that is still with us today and has come to be known as a Ponzi scheme—a scam flexible enough to adapt to changes in society and simple enough to stand the test of time. It is also effective enough to have cheated people for almost a hundred years with no sign of slowing down.

In essence, the Ponzi scheme is the classic pyramid scam—an investment advisor claims to be getting really good returns on your money when, in fact, he or she is merely taking money from newer investors to pay the early investors outlandish interest rates so that they generate the word of mouth needed to get the next wave of investors. It is a house of cards destined to collapse, usually with the originator long gone by the time most of the victims try and fail to get the money back.

During the early 1900s, postal reply coupons were used to permit someone sending mail to a person in a foreign country to furnish means for a reply instead of requiring the recipient of the letter to pay for return postage. An American businessman, for example, could send a contract

> The simple scam of paying off early investors with the money of later investors continues to this day.

to his or her counterpart in the United Kingdom along with a postal reply coupon to cover the cost of sending the contract back to America.

Through what appeared to be a rather complicated transaction similar to currency trading today, Ponzi purported to convert his American dollars into currencies in other countries with favorable exchange rates and purchase postal reply coupons in those countries at a profit. To finance this project on a large scale, Ponzi sought out investors, promising them a 50 percent return on their investment in only 45 days. Initial investors were paid off handsomely, and the word got out that this man was a financial wizard. More and more people invested. At the height of his scheme, investors poured money into Ponzi's scheme at a rate of $250,000 a day.

Unfortunately for Ponzi, his success was not long lived. Investigative reporters, along with state and federal officials, were looking into Ponzi's investment company. Perhaps the most telling piece of information came out in a newspaper article published in the *Boston Post* that said the number of postal reply coupons equal to the money invested in the scheme would have had to be 160,000,000 coupons, whereas the total number of postal reply coupons in the world was only 27,000. Soon thereafter, Ponzi's empire crumbled, and eventually he pleaded guilty to mail fraud and was sent to prison.

Finally, the truth of Ponzi's scheme became clear. He would take the investment money of later investors to pay the promised returns to earlier investors. This, in turn, would lure more and more investors to him. However, his scheme was ultimately doomed to failure by simple mathematics, because there just were not enough people to keep this scheme or any such scheme going forever.

Ponzi had made one great mistake. A good conman knows when to leave. Ponzi did not. His greed kept him in Boston right up until the time of his arrest. Charles Ponzi's short reign as the king of the scams was over, but like the events around Boston in 1776, Ponzi's scam was the scam heard 'round the world. His scheme has been repeated with just slight variations for nearly 100 years. The form of investment changes from time to time, but the simple scam of paying off early investors with the money of later investors continues to this day.

View promises of outlandish returns on investments with great skepticism.

Our teachers used to implore us to do our homework, and nowhere is that more important than in evaluating investment opportunities. The truth is, if it sounds too good to be true, it usually is. View promises of outlandish returns on investments with great skepticism. Don't let greed make you less vigilant. As Charles Ponzi's later investors learned, just because earlier investors saw great profits does not mean that you will see profits or even a return of your initial investment.

TRUTH

Chain letters

Aretha Franklin was right when she sang the song "Chain of Fools," because anyone who gets involved with a chain letter is a fool. Like many scams, chain letters have been around for a long time. People have been losing money to chain letters since 1888. The scam is tweaked now and then to look a bit different or even to make it appear legal, but the bottom line is that a chain letter is not a love letter, and it is never legal.

At its essence, a chain letter involves a letter that you receive containing a list of people, commonly five. You are asked to send a certain sum of money to the first person on the list, take her name off of the list, add your name as the last numbered person on the list, and send the list to five more people with the same instructions.

The attraction of chain letters is easy to understand. It is simple to do and promises enormous wealth for little effort. The problem is not just that it is illegal, but that it is doomed to fail.

Let's start by looking at the math—something I have been loathe to do since junior high school days, but something that begrudgingly I must admit comes in handy sometimes. If every one of the typically five people appearing on a chain letter had followed the instructions and sent the letter to five of their friends (not that a true friend would ever involve you in a chain letter), by the time you receive it, the chain letter would have had to sustain itself through 3,905 people or links on the chain. And that is assuming that the chain began with the person who is listed first on the chain letter that you receive. If everyone had followed the instructions precisely and a person who had just been just bumped from the list initiated the chain, the number of people involved in the chain letter rises to 19,530. And that begins to tell you why chain letters are illegal. Chain letters are a pyramid scheme that will fail as

> The attraction of chain letters is easy to understand. It is simple to do and promises enormous wealth for little effort. The problem is not just that it is illegal, but that it is doomed to fail.

we run out of people on the planet. It is impossible for a chain letter ever to fulfill its promise to everyone participating.

Those ethically challenged people who do not care that eventually the chain letter must fail as long as they receive significant money in the early stages of the letter should consider the real possibility that people receiving the chain letter will not follow the instructions exactly but will insert their name at the top of the list rather than at the bottom. They also might even change all the names on the list so that they are just aliases of themselves, thus putting themselves on the list in five different ways. Either way, you do not move up the list, and you do not get money. Or perhaps the people to whom you send the chain letter follow the instructions exactly with one notable exception: They do not send money. No matter how you look at it, Aretha was right: Chain letters are for fools.

In one famous incident, the Federal Trade Commission sent out its own mass mailing to 2,000 people who had participated in an Internet chain letter that promised participants a minimum of $46,000 in 90 days if they did not break the chain. The FTC letter warned participants in the letter that chain letters that involve money are illegal. Even if you did not originate the chain letter, but merely participated, you have violated the law. The chain letter that caught the attention of the FTC was pretty much the standard chain letter. However, what made it somewhat unique was an attempt to make it appear to be legal through a provision that the money contributed to the chain letter participants was in return for something of value. Interestingly enough, in this case, the something of value was instructions on how to start your own chain letter over the Internet.

It is important to remember that chain letters are always illegal. As was the situation with the chain letter that prompted the mass mailing by the Federal Trade Commission to known participants, sometimes chain letters will be disguised to resemble a legitimate business proposition by selling you some inexpensive item, but the essence of any chain letter is the pyramid scheme that drives it. It does not take the proverbial rocket scientist to see the characteristics of a chain letter even when disguised as a business.

> The essence of any chain letter is the pyramid scheme that drives it.

Don't fall prey to claims that appear in some chain letters that the U.S. Postal Service has given its endorsement of that particular chain letter and ruled it as legal. The truth is, the U.S. Postal Service does not do that. If you see such a claim, you need read no further to determine that you are dealing with an illegal chain letter.

TRUTH

A couple of the basics

Pyramid schemes

Pyramid schemes have probably been with us since the pyramids in Egypt were being built. This particular scam gets its name from an image of the scam, with the originator of the scam at the apex of the pyramid and an ever-increasing number of participants (and ultimately victims) fanning out from the top. For example, if one person who recruited ten people to pay him started the pyramid, and each of the ten recruits in turn recruited ten more people to pay them, after eleven rounds, the number of people required to sustain the pyramid would exceed the Earth's population. And therein lies the scam. Ultimately, the pyramid must fall, and people will lose their money.

At its essence, a pyramid scheme is a fraudulent, unsustainable business model in which people receive money through enrolling new people in the scheme who, in turn, receive money from enrolling more people in the scheme. No financially equivalent product or service is received for the enrollment fees, the only return on "investment" comes from bringing more people into the scheme. Chain letters are a form of a pyramid scheme.

As with chain letters, pyramid schemes prey upon people's greed and a desire for easy money, common human traits that invite scammers. As with chain letters, pyramid schemes have managed to evolve in a manner that even Charles Darwin would have found amazing as they change the terminology and the format to make them appear legal. Sometimes they are called investment clubs or gifting networks, but it is easy to see that they are pyramid schemes. One recent version of a pyramid scheme involved a "gifting club" in which people made cash "gifts" to higher ranking members of the club with the promise that as they recruited new members to the club, they would rise through the ranks of the club until they reached a position where they themselves would be receiving substantial "gifts" from

> Pyramid schemes have managed to evolve in a manner that even Charles Darwin would have found amazing as they change the terminology and the format to make them appear legal.

newer members of the club. The truth is, pyramid schemes are always an illegal and losing proposition.

One complicating factor with pyramid schemes is their close resemblance to multilevel marketing practices. We are all familiar with multilevel marketing companies such as Mary Kay Cosmetics, Tupperware, Amway, and Avon, which use a network of independent distributors to sell various consumer products. In multilevel marketing, you can obtain income from the efforts of members of your sales team who, in turn, can have their own sales teams from which they obtain income. However, money is not earned merely by recruiting new people to the company. A simple way to distinguish a legitimate multilevel marketing company from a disguised pyramid scheme is that with a pyramid scheme, actual sales of products, if any, are small. The money is made from signing up new members regardless of the amount of product sold. Generally, the fees to become involved in a legitimate multilevel marketing company enterprise are small, whereas the fees involved with joining a pyramid scheme may be substantial. Another key way to distinguish between legitimate multilevel marketing companies is that legitimate companies that require you to purchase inventory generally buy back unsold inventory if you leave the business. Pyramid schemes will not.

Pyramid scheme scammers are clever. They never call their con a pyramid scheme because they understand that we all know that those are illegal. Instead, they may go under the name of investment clubs or gift clubs. Often, they will even have a completely worthless letter supposedly issued by the IRS or a legal opinion from a law firm or even the FTC indicating that this particular club is legal and not a pyramid scheme. The truth is, these supporting pieces of documentation are just another piece of the fraud.

> They may go under the name of investment clubs or gift clubs.

Bait and switch

A bait and switch scam occurs when you are lured by advertising to purchase a particular product but then steered toward buying a different, usually more expensive product. This scam at one time or another has victimized almost everyone, which is why federal regulations prohibit the practice.

The fact is, bait and switch remains one of the slimier forms of deception. Show you a beautiful car, and sell you a more expensive car—which the seller convinces you will better meet your needs. The truth is, you should be wary any time a vendor brings you in with an advertisement to purchase a particular product but then discourages you from buying that particular product, instead urging you to buy another "better" product. Even if ultimately, before purchase, you are told the facts regarding the products, the mere attracting you to the seller through this deceptive form of advertising is illegal.

TRUTH

14

Nigerian scam

A staple of the Internet and omnipresent in everyone's email is the Nigerian scam. Although it has many variations, a common version of it is an unsolicited email that you receive from someone in Nigeria who tells you that the sender needs to transfer large amounts of money out of Nigeria and needs your help.

Although this scam is now commenced primarily through email, the scam itself is an oldie that dates back to 1588 when it was known as the "Spanish Prisoner con." In those days, a letter was sent to the victim purportedly from someone on behalf of a wealthy aristocrat who was imprisoned in Spain under a false name. The identity of the nobleman was not revealed for security reasons, but the victim was asked to help raise money to obtain the release of the aristocrat, who, it was promised, would reward the money-contributing victim with great sums of money and, in some versions of the con, the Spanish prisoner's beautiful daughter in marriage.

In its most recent incarnation, you are promised great sums of money if you assist a Nigerian in his effort to transfer money out of his country. Variations include the movement of embezzled funds by corrupt officials, a dying gentleman who wants to make charitable gifts, or a minor bank official who is trying to move the money of deceased foreigners out of his bank without the government taking it. One popular variation of the scam involves an email from a lawyer informing you that there was a plane crash in Nigeria in which a wealthy person died. The lawyer represents the estate of the plane crash victim, who, you are told, has the same surname as you. Due to complicated Nigerian law, the millions contained in the estate will revert to the government unless it can be transferred to you as an heir. For your trouble, you are promised millions of dollars, with the remaining money to go to charity. However, you soon learn that you need to send money to the lawyer for various fees, bribes, insurance, and other costs before you get your inheritance that never comes.

The essence of the Nigerian scam is a promise of a huge reward for payments that you make in advance of the ultimate payout. But the payout never comes.

The essence of the Nigerian scam is a promise of a huge reward for payments that you make in advance of the ultimate payout. But the payout never comes.

Many of us would immediately look at such an email with a chuckle, secure in the belief that such a proposal must be a scam. But thousands of people have fallen for this con. Some, who make the mistake of thinking that they are smarter than the scammers, try to do their own "due diligence" and find what appear to be actual places of business and even apparent contacts at government offices. On the surface, which is what the scammers are counting on, the ridiculous scam looks like it might even be legitimate. It never is. Once the victim has initially agreed to take part in this mutual effort to move funds, often after receiving what appear to be official documents, the victim finds that the deal is not as simple as it originally appeared. Complications arise. Government or bank officials need to be bribed. Lawyers need to be paid. The victim is asked to contribute money, often as a loan to the enterprise. You can guess what happens next. The victim sends money to advance what he or she thinks is a big payout but finds that the only payout involves the funds sent to the scammers. After they have received the victim's money, the scammers suddenly stop communicating and vanish. However, in some instances, adding insult to injury, once the well has gone dry and the victim has stopped sending money, the scammers use the information they have obtained about the victim during the con to victimize them a second time through identity theft.

The scammers use the information they have obtained about the victim during the con to victimize them a second time through identity theft.

One thing to look for immediately is the email address of the person sending you the initial communication. Although they often purport to be associated with a bank, the email address will not be that of a bank, but rather a private email address. But the best course of action is to just ignore an email that you know in your heart is a scam.

TRUTH

Who knew?
A flurry of old champs

Travel fraud

Like many other scams, travel fraud often starts with your being notified that you have won a contest that you never entered. This time the prize is a terrific vacation trip.

You may learn of your winning through a telemarketer, an email, a fax, or a postcard. The "free" trip that you have won usually comes with fees that are barely visible in the fine print. Hidden charges, conditions, and additional fees that you must pay to get the free trip can add up quickly. Often, you are asked for your credit card number or bank account information, sometimes just for identification purposes; however, the identification purpose is just to identify you as a sucker. Other times, you are required to pay a good faith deposit for your free trip that you lose when it becomes impossible to schedule your trip.

Another vacation travel scam is an offer that you receive, often by fax, that has a too-good-to-be-true price for a great vacation. And it is indeed too good to be true. Generally, the hotel accommodations are pretty bad, and it may cost you dearly to upgrade. In addition, scheduling the vacation for the time you wish may carry extra fees. Remember, you get what you pay for.

You get what you pay for.

Charity scams

Particularly around holiday time or when there's been a tragic storm (a tsunami or Katrina), scammers take advantage of our charitable nature and solicit by mail, in person, and on the phone for phony charities. Often the names of the phony charity may be amazingly similar to a legitimate charity, but the money that you give to this "charity" does not end up advancing legitimate charitable activities but merely finds its way to the pockets of clever scammers. An independent problem that arises even when you make a contribution to a so-called "legitimate" charity is when that charity takes most of your donation and spends it "administratively" or on more fund raising efforts rather than applying the money directly to charitable actions. Always check out the charity to which you give to determine not just if it is legitimate but also how much of what the charity receives actually is applied to charitable works. Go to the website www.nasconet.org to get a link to the regulators of charities in your particular state. You can also get financial information on specific charities at GuideStar at www.guidestar.org, the Better Business Bureau's Wise Giving Alliance at www.give.org, the American Institute of Philanthropy at www.charitywatch.org, or Charity Navigator at www.charitynavigator.org.

It's common for charities to hire professional fund-raisers to manage their fund-raising. There is nothing illegal or improper about this practice. But you may want to ask if the person contacting you is a professional fund-raiser and what percentage of your donation the fund-raiser will keep. If you are uncomfortable with this arrangement, you may want to send your check (never send cash) directly to the charity to ensure that the charity gets the full benefit of your donation. If the charitable solicitor offers to send a courier or an overnight delivery service to pick up your donation, beware! That is characteristic of a scam.

If you are contacted on the phone by a charity, play it safe and ask the charity to send you written material for you to evaluate the particular charity. Even if you have registered on the national Do Not Call list to avoid telemarketing calls, the law still permits you to be solicited on the phone by charities directly. However, as with any telemarketing call, the truth is, you have no way of knowing on the phone if the person you are speaking to is legitimate or a scammer. Play it safe, and never give out personal information or your credit card number to anyone who calls you on the phone.

You should be aware that when it comes to donations to charitable organizations, "tax exempt" and "tax deductible" are not the same thing. A "charitable" organization may be tax exempt and not be required to pay income taxes. However, your payment to such an organization is not automatically "tax deductible" as a charitable gift on your income tax return. Just because an organization is non-profit and, therefore, tax exempt does not mean that your gift is tax deductible to you. Only gifts to charitable organizations that receive their tax exemption through section 501(c)(3) of the Internal Revenue Code are tax deductible. You can confirm that the charity you contribute to is one to which gifts are tax deductible by going to the IRS website at www.irs.gov/charities.

Staged auto accidents

You get cut off in traffic by a car that suddenly stops, and although you slam on your brakes, you rear-end the car that just cut you off. You attempt to merge into a line of traffic and are waved in by a helpful driver whose car you collide into when he then doesn't let you into the lane. You are driving close to (or perhaps slightly over) your lane line when you get side swiped by another car. You are going through an intersection when another car coming from a different direction hits your car. Not all automobile accidents are accidents. Sometimes they are staged as a way of defrauding insurance companies or you. In each of the previously described scenarios, the scammers will have phony victims and phony witnesses to bolster their stories that the accident was your fault. Sometimes they may suddenly turn into your best friend and be willing to just settle with you for cash rather than involve the insurance companies. This may even seem like a good offer because it avoids insurance complications (see www.fbi.gov/page2/feb05/stagedauto021805.htm).

When you exchange license and registration information, be mindful not to provide more information than required that can be used for identity theft purposes.

The truth is, this settlement is not a good offer. It is a scam. If you are involved in an automobile accident, call the police. When you exchange license and registration information, be mindful not to provide more information than required that can be used for identity theft purposes. Report all accidents to your insurance company and do not pay a cash settlement at the scene. Get the license and registration of the other driver and take down the pertinent information. Do not merely accept his offer to you of this information written down on a piece of paper. Make sure you see the actual license and registration.

TRUTH

More reasons to be wary

Lost pets

Emotion, fear, and concern are allies of scammers, and all three elements are present when a pet owner has lost a beloved pet.

Taking advantage of this situation, scammers who notice fliers put up by owners of missing pets or who read online postings of missing pets contact the owners and tell them that they have found their wandering pet and will be happy to ship the pet back to the owner as soon as the owner sends sufficient money to cover the shipping costs. Often there will be a follow-up communication that looks like it is from a legitimate shipping company confirming the initial communication.

The truth is, it is a scam. If you are contacted as a potential victim, ask for a picture of your pet to be sent. You can say that you merely want to confirm that it is your pet. Or if it is a parrot, you can ask to speak to the bird.

The old gray mare—the gray market

The old gray mare just ain't what she used to be—and often, neither are products that you may buy on the gray market. Everyone is aware of the term black market, which refers to items that have been stolen and then resold, sometimes to unwary consumers and other times to consumers who know full well that they are buying stolen goods but do not seem to be particularly bothered by this fact.

Goods such as electronic equipment sold throughout the world sell at different prices based on differences in currency valuations as well as market conditions in the particular country. Entrepreneurs, looking to make a buck and take advantage of these fluctuations in prices worldwide, buy up large quantities of goods such as cameras or electronic equipment and then sell the items online here in America. It has been estimated by the Alliance for Gray Market and Counterfeit Abatement that about 40 billion dollars' worth of technological products are sold on the gray market annually throughout the world.

One problem with items purchased on the gray market is that often the manufacturers of the products do not honor warranties on gray market products. In fact, some manufacturers will not even service these unauthorized imported goods not sold by an authorized retailer. Whether it is on eBay or other online auction sites, gray market goods often are readily available online. However, when you buy gray market goods from a seller with whom you are not familiar, not only can you not be sure that any manufacturer's warranty will be honored, but also sometimes, less than honest merchants even substitute cheap components for more expensive parts of the item you purchase.

So, how do you protect yourself and feel confident that the deal you are getting is good but not too good? Make sure the item comes with a full warranty. This is particularly important with electronic equipment and cameras. Get a serial number and check with the manufacturer to confirm that it is indeed under warranty. The seller may insist that the product is covered by a warranty, and maybe it is, but you can never be sure when you are not dealing directly with the manufacturer that the warranty offered is legitimate and will be honored. Make sure there are no hidden fees that jack up the price for expensive parts that should be included with the product, and make sure that you know who you are dealing with.*

Hotel scam

People have come to expect things to go wrong. It is Murphy's Law that whatever can go wrong will go wrong. There is even a common expression that tells us that "Fecal matter happens," although not precisely in those words. And that is why people are so susceptible to the scam in which, as a hotel guest, you get a call to your room from the front desk or the manager that there is a problem with the credit card you used when you checked into the hotel. You are asked to verify your credit card number over the phone, which unfortunately some people do. Shortly thereafter, charges are made to your credit card that you never authorized.

The truth is, the caller is not the manager or anyone else from the hotel. The call is from a scammer. The first thing to remember is that no hotel employee will ever ask you for your credit card over the phone. If, somehow, there were a problem with your credit card, you would be asked to come to the front desk. The rule in a hotel is the same as the rule anywhere: Never give out personal information of any kind to anyone whom you have not called unless you have verified whom you are speaking to. In a hotel, you should call the manager of the hotel directly.

---

* Kessler, Michelle. "Bargain Sounds Too Good? Stay Away." USA Today. Dec 10, 2006.

Adoption scam

A sad fact is that when people are the most vulnerable and trusting, they are more likely to become a victim of a scam. So it should come as no surprise that people seeking to adopt a child have been a common target of scammers.

There are many different scams involving adoptions that never are completed but where the prospective adoptive parents lose considerable money to scammers arranging these phony adoptions. Many adoption scams originate online, where it is cheap and easy to establish a website and a presence at little cost that appears to be legitimate but, in fact, is not. Sometimes the scammer promises, for a fee, to bring together birth mothers willing to put their children up for adoption with adoptive parents. In many instances, there are no birth mothers; in other instances, these birth mothers promise their babies to multiple adoptive parents. Many of the phony adoptions involve babies born in foreign countries. This scam plays on an additional vulnerability of people wanting to adopt—namely, that they are unfamiliar with the laws of these foreign countries.

The truth is, adoption is a complicated matter. You should deal only with agencies that are licensed in your state. In addition, you should not take for granted a license document or license number provided to you by the adoption agency. Check with your state's adoption regulatory agency. You should also not rely on the Internet as your sole resource for adoption information and assistance. Meet the person offering to help you at his or her office to see for yourself if there even *is* an office. Surrogate parent adoptions are particularly complicated and fertile ground for scams. You should never consider a surrogate parent adoption without being represented by a lawyer familiar with this complicated and evolving area of the law. For international adoptions, check with the State Department about the regulations for adoption in the country where you are considering adopting. The State Department's Office of Children's Issues in the Bureau of Consular Affairs has many helpful brochures that deal with foreign adoptions. Finally, hire a lawyer to assist you. International adoptions are intricate and complicated.

TRUTH

17

And you thought you'd heard it all

Affinity fraud

We tend to trust people who are just like us. That is a truism. With a knowledge of psychology that would make Sigmund Freud envious, conmen use that trust to their advantage. Scammers know that once they have a potential victim's heart and trust, their wallets soon follow.

We are experiencing an epidemic of fraud that targets particular nationalities, ethnic groups, racial groups, fraternal organizations, and religious groups. Religion-related scams are particularly common. A scam artist may join a particular church, synagogue, or mosque and gain the trust and confidence of the congregants or even the religious leader of the congregation by making a significant contribution to the religious organization. But this is just seed money. Scammers often target members of a religious, ethnic, fraternal, or other group that they appear to belong to and offer "special" investment opportunities that ultimately turn out to be worthless. Often, to sweeten the pot, particularly in a religious affinity group scam, the scammer tells the charitably inclined victims that a portion of the profits of his investment program will be used for a charitable purpose near and dear to the hearts of the victims. Sometimes the fraud is organized as a Ponzi deal so that people in your church, synagogue, social organization, or community group become the unwitting accomplices of the scam artist who ends up making the initial victims of the scams his best salespeople as they recommend the particular investment that has, at least initially, worked so well for them.

The truth is, you should never trust anyone who asks you to trust him. Trust me. Always do your homework before you invest your money. The endorsement of someone you know and trust is no substitute for real research into any investment.

> Always do your homework before you invest your money. The endorsement of someone you know and trust is no substitute for real research into any investment.

Psychics

Letters, emails, or telephone calls from psychics either offering good fortune or the ending of bad fortune are common scams. The positive psychic scam occurs when the psychic promises to share a secret with you that will bring you fame and fortune. Often the psychic offers to sell you a special good luck charm that is guaranteed to make good fortune smile upon you. Sometimes this particular scam is coupled with a lottery scam by which, shortly after purchasing the requisite good luck charm, you receive a notice that you have just won a lottery. Unfortunately, this is just another scam in which you are required to send an advance payment to receive your lottery winnings. Paying for a worthless good luck charm and then sending in money to claim a nonexistent prize is a double whammy. The negative psychic scam occurs when you are told that you are in danger from a demonic force and that if you do not send money to the psychic to ward off this force, something terrible will happen to you.

The truth is, if you want to believe in psychics, it's your business, but when you receive an unsolicited email or letter from someone claiming to be a psychic, I predict it is just a scam.

One last word on psychics. Many people remember the Psychic Friends Network, which was a service by which you could talk with a psychic on the telephone for $3.99 per minute. At the height of its popularity, the Psychic Friends Network professed to have more than 2,000 psychics available to take your call. The service was advertised extensively in television infomercials during the early 1990s, many of which were hosted by singer Dionne Warwick. After it raked in more than $100,000,000 dollars of profits, the company landed in bankruptcy in 1998 due to a combination of bad management and competition from other psychic services. I wonder if any of the psychics saw it coming.

> If you want to believe in psychics, it's your business, but when you receive an unsolicited email or letter from someone claiming to be a psychic, I predict it is just a scam.

Voter registration fraud

The Bible says that to everything there is a season. Scammers also are aware of seasons when it comes to fresh opportunities for scamming you. During hurricane season, you can expect to be hit for a charitable contribution to victims of particular storms by scammers pretending to be legitimate charities. During Super Bowl season, scams offering phony Super Bowl tickets and travel packages are common. And during election years, you may expect to get a call from a scammer pretending to be from either your local voter registration board or a civic organization offering to either help you register to vote or to confirm your status as an enrolled voter. After the initial pitch, the scammer asks you for information to confirm your identity, such as your Social Security number. Some scammers are even so audacious as to ask for a credit card number.

> Legitimate voter registration drives are not generally done over the phone, and they will never ask you for personal information.

The truth is, this is a scam. The information is being gathered not to register you to vote, but to register you as a victim of identity theft, because the scammer is taking your personal information to make you a victim of identity theft. Legitimate voter registration drives are not generally done over the phone, and they will never ask you for personal information. As always, follow the rule of not giving out personal identifying information on the telephone to anyone whom you have not called and are not sure who they are.

TRUTH

18

Money lost, borrowed, or gambled

Unclaimed property

You are told through an email or other communication that there are billions of dollars of unclaimed or abandoned money being held by the states and federal government and that some of this money is yours. For a fee, this helpful person will assist you in locating your property and claiming it.

The truth is, various state and federal agencies are indeed holding more than 24 billion dollars of unclaimed money that is waiting to be retrieved by the rightful owners. State law requires financial institutions, such as banks, to turn over money from inactive accounts. Typical abandoned property includes savings or checking accounts, stocks, uncashed dividend checks, certificates of deposit, and utility security deposits.

The illegal scam involving unclaimed property begins when you receive an email or other notice from a company that promises to do a free search on your behalf to locate any money that is being held by the government as abandoned property. You are told that all you have to do is call the company's 809 number for more information. The first piece of information that you may not know is that by calling the 809 number, you incur a charge on your telephone bill. The call is not free. Then, in response to your call, the illegal scammers merely send you some useless general information while they inform you that you need to pay a membership fee or some other sort of fee before the search can proceed.

The legal scam involving unclaimed property occurs when you are contacted by a legitimate company that searches public records of the data banks of the individual state agencies holding unclaimed or abandoned property to identify people who may have property to be claimed. Once the company has identified these people, it contacts them and offers to help them through the process for a fee. However, due to privacy regulations, although the company contacting you may have general information that indicates that property of yours is being held by the state, the company does not know for sure if you are the true owner of the property and doesn't know the value of the property being held. Most importantly, and why I believe that this is just a legal scam, all the information that you need to find property of yours that may be held by the government as unclaimed or abandoned property is available online at no charge to you. These companies cannot do anything that you cannot readily do for yourself.

The best place to begin your search for lost property being held by each of the 50 states is to go to the website of the National Association of Unclaimed Property Administrators at www.unclaimed. org. This website can link you to your own state's agency that deals with unclaimed or abandoned property. Some other useful websites that can help you find lost money are www.irs.gov, which is the website of the IRS to which you can go to find tax refund money you may be owed, and www.pbgc.gov, which is the website of the Pension Benefit Guaranty Corporation, a federal agency that holds unclaimed pension funds.

Loan scam

It's easy to get a loan if you don't need the money. However, if you really need the money, a low credit score may make it difficult to borrow from your local bank or credit union. Scammers take advantage of desperate borrowers through advertisements for phony loan companies with official sounding names, such as "B & T Financial Group," offering loans that are easy to qualify for even if your credit score is low. You provide your personal information in a credit application by phone, mail, or online. You are then told that if you wire a money order of between $500 and $1,000 for processing fees, your loan will be approved, and your money will be on its way.

The truth is, this is a scam. The only money that is on its way is the money that you send to the scammer. And, to make matters worse, not only will you lose the money you send for processing fees, but also the information you provide may lead to identity theft that may make you a victim a second time. The telltale clue in this, as in so many scams, is the advance fee payment. Legitimate lenders usually deduct fees from the loan amount. Do your homework, and check with your local Better Business Bureau and the consumer protection division of your state's Attorney General before sending any personal information or money to an unfamiliar lender.

Gambling scam

As long as there have been people, there has been gambling. Early cave drawings depict gambling. Gambling with dice was popular in the Roman Empire. And, as long as there has been gambling, there has been someone either cheating or scamming people with a "system" that is touted to enable people to break the laws of probability.

The truth is, with the exception of Blackjack, the math is always in favor of the casino. And even with Blackjack, to exploit a potential slim mathematical advantage, it takes the brain of an MIT student, as shown by the success (for a while) of the famous MIT Blackjack team during the 1990s that beat the casinos for millions of dollars. Their system involved a sophisticated card counting system that determined when a significant number of high cards remained in the deck that would provide a slight mathematical edge to the card playing team member. Such a system is technically legal if no device or calculator is used at the Blackjack table. But it also takes the mind of an MIT student to pull it off.

A typical gambling scam is one that offers to sell you a system that can be used to win at the casinos. Playing on our memory of the MIT Blackjack team, the system offered is often said to have been designed by a mathematical scholar. Generally, the systems are merely variations of a strategy that goes back to French gamblers in the 1700s called the Martingale betting system. At its most basic, the strategy requires the gambler to double his bet after every loss so that in his first win, he will recover all his previous losses along with a profit. To the mathematically unsophisticated, this may seem somewhat attractive both in its simplicity to understand as well as the complex mathematical formulas that are purported to support this strategy. The truth is, this strategy would work only if you had an unlimited amount of money with which to gamble. Gambling systems that guarantee success are a scam. They always have been, and they always will be. You can bet on it.

TRUTH

Lottery and contest scams

Conmen know that everyone loves to win a prize. As a result, phony prize scams are rampant. It is hard enough to win a prize when you have entered a legitimate sweepstakes, but when you are notified that you have won a contest that you never even entered, you should be hearing "Danger Will Robinson" ringing in your head even if you never watched the old television show *Lost in Space*.

One form of a contest prize scam requires you to buy something to qualify for the prize that you have "won." Generally, the things you are required to buy are particularly overpriced when compared to the prize that you have supposedly won.

Another common lottery scam involves up-front fees that you are required to pay to claim your terrific prize. Knowing that some people might be initially skeptical of being told that they have won a prize in an international lottery that they did not enter, one particular scam came in the form of an email purportedly from the FBI. The message line in your email read "FBI Internet Fraud Watch/Alert," and the return email address gained people's confidence by appearing as FBIfraudalert@hotmail.co.uk or FBIfraudwatch@hotmail.co.uk. The truth is, it was a scam. The email told you that you had won a big prize in a lottery sponsored by a large, familiar company such as Microsoft or MasterCard, and the lottery had been examined by both the FBI and Scotland Yard and determined to be legitimate. You were also told that the lottery funds were insured. So who wouldn't send in a processing fee when both the FBI and Scotland Yard have assured you that the lottery is legitimate? Someone thinking clearly. Don't let your greed overrule your brain. Never trust an email to be from whom it says it is from. The FBI does not work with or endorse particular lotteries.

> Never trust an email to be from whom it says it is from. The FBI does not work with or endorse particular lotteries.

Many people who received a check from Clorox, the bleach company, indicating that it was part of the "American Lottery Sweepstakes" may have merely thought that this was a legitimate advertising promotion. Along with the check and a congratulatory letter, the victims received instructions to wire money (always a danger signal in scams) to a Canadian clearinghouse to cover the fees for processing the prize money. The truth is, this, too, is a scam. You don't win contests that you have not entered. You don't have to pay fees to receive winnings in legitimate sweepstakes. And you should never consider any check as real money, regardless of how legitimate it looks, until the funds have not only been deposited in your account, but also the check has actually cleared. As for money that you wire to the scammer while his check is in the process of bouncing; that money is gone forever.

Another form of prize scam involves the income taxes due on prize winnings. As with many scams, there is just enough of a kernel of truth in this assertion to make an unsuspecting victim susceptible to the scam. Lottery and contest winnings are generally subject to income taxes; however, the operators of scam lotteries tell you that you must pay *them* the income tax due on your prize. The truth is, you pay the tax on your prize winnings either directly to the IRS through an estimated tax payment, or the taxes are deducted from the prize before you receive it, in which case you would receive a Form 1099 from the sponsor of the sweepstakes informing you of the amount already deducted for your income taxes. Never pay income taxes to the sponsor of a lottery or other contest.

> Operators of scam lotteries tell you that you must pay *them* the income tax due on your prize.

In another variation of the lottery scam, you may be sent a check for a portion of your winnings along with directions to send back money for processing fees. Unfortunately, the check from the phony lottery bounces, but your check back to the scammer does not. Adding insult to injury, some people who have fallen for this scam not only lost the money they sent to the scammer for processing fees but also were charged overdraft fees by their own bank when they bounced checks assuming that they had the prize money in their bank account.

Another lottery scam occurs when the scammer buys a lottery ticket choosing the winning numbers from the previous day's or week's lottery drawing. He then alters the date on the ticket to make it appear to be a winning ticket. Next, he approaches you with a sob story explaining why he cannot collect the money. Perhaps he is going through a divorce. Perhaps he is ineligible to claim the prize; this scam works particularly well with scammers who may appear to be teenagers. Whatever the reason, the result is the same: They offer to sell you the ticket so that you can collect the prize, and they get a significantly reduced amount of money from you. It's a win-win solution, if you ever saw one. The truth is, buying a lottery ticket from anyone who is not in the business is a sucker's bet. You can't win.

> Buying a lottery ticket from anyone who is not in the business is a sucker's bet.

TRUTH

Exercise scams

> e are never deceived;
> we deceive ourselves.
>
> —Johann Wolfgang von Goethe

A common feature of many exercise scams takes advantage of our desire to get in better shape with the least effort possible. Unfortunately, you are left with a program that often is expensive and doesn't come close to the representations in the print advertisements or infomercials that prompted you to buy the product.

The truth is, exercise takes effort. There are many forms of exercise that can be enjoyable and not too taxing. There are tremendous benefits to just a regular walking program. In fact, the key to a successful exercise program is to find something that you enjoy doing and feel comfortable fitting into your regular, daily routine. This is the only way you will stick with an exercise program for the period required to get into shape and maintain a healthy body weight. Too many pieces of exercise equipment are gathering dust or are used to hang clothes on after purchasers did not incorporate the particular exercise equipment into their daily lives.

One thing that all exercise scams have in common is exaggerated, overstated claims that we know in our hearts, not to mention our biceps, are too good to be true. If an exercise program or machine promises amazingly swift results without effort or promises to burn off fat from a particular part of your body, such as your waist or your buttocks, you should know the program is a scam.

Forget about the testimonials in the advertisements. The fine print may even tell you that the results achieved by these people may not be typical. If you are considering an exercise program, talk with your physician or a certified trainer at a local gymnasium before buying a program or a particular piece of exercise equipment.

When you evaluate the price of the particular exercise equipment or program, look at the total price. How many "easy" monthly payments do you have to make? How much is the shipping and handling going to cost you? What are the delivery charges? What are the sales taxes? Exercise your mind and a little caution before you buy exercise equipment.

And don't forget: The money-back guarantee for a scam exercise product is as much of a scam as the product itself. It is worthless. The truth is, you should never rely on the guarantees of a company you're not totally familiar with.

TRUTH

Weight loss scams

Many of us need to drop a few pounds. Fortunately, losing weight is not particularly complicated. Eat a healthy diet with reasonable portions and exercise regularly. It's simple, but not that easy. Many of us want a quick, easy way to lose weight. The market for weight loss programs and products is huge. The advertisements are compelling, often using celebrities we're familiar with who proclaim the effectiveness of the particular weight loss product. Generally, these products share two important characteristics: They're easy to use, and they're not particularly effective.

In January 2007, the Federal Trade Commission (FTC) settled claims against four major marketers of weight loss products. Pursuant to the settlement, the companies Xenadrine EFX, CortiSlim, TrimSpa, and One-A-Day WeightSmart agreed to pay the government $25 million in fines as well as not to misrepresent studies purporting to support their products' weight loss claims. They also agreed to stop their deceptive advertising. It should be noted that, consistent with similar settlements negotiated by the FTC, although all four companies agreed to forfeit substantial money and agreed to change their product claims, the companies officially denied that they had done any of the things they were accused of. In effect, the companies were permitted to say that they didn't do anything wrong, but they promised not to do it again.

> Generally, [weight loss] products share two important characteristics: They're easy to use, and they're not particularly effective.

In the case of Xenadrine EFX, it was disclosed by the FTC that none of the studies commissioned by the company showed that using the product brought about substantial weight loss. In fact, in one of the studies, the users of Xenadrine EFX lost an average of 1.5 pounds over the entire ten-week duration of the study, while the control group that received a placebo lost 2.5 pounds during the same period. There is nothing like a good placebo. In addition, the FTC also alleged that the slim, attractive people whose "before and after" pictures were used in the advertisements actually lost weight through rigorous exercise and diet rather than merely popping Xenadrine EFX tablets.

The lesson with weight loss products is to be skeptical. The truth is, there are no quick fixes. Here are a few rules to remember when evaluating weight loss products and programs.

- Be wary of any weight loss product that is sold exclusively either over the Internet or through mail-order advertisements.

- Don't believe the claims of any weight loss product or program that promises that you can lose tremendous amounts of weight quickly without dieting or exercise.

- No cream that you rub into your skin can help you lose substantial weight.

- No product can block the absorption of fat or calories. There is no magic potion that will help you lose weight while still eating a high-calorie diet.

- Spot reducing of hips, thighs, or anywhere else is impossible.

Just because you see a product advertised in a legitimate newspaper, magazine, or television infomercial does not mean that the product is legitimate.

The Food and Drug Administration (FDA) and the FTC are continually taking action against the scammers who operate phony diet programs and products, but their chances of keeping every phony diet program and product off the market are slim. Just because you see a product advertised in a legitimate newspaper, magazine, or television infomercial does not mean that the product is legitimate. The best course of action is to ask your physician about the effectiveness of a particular weight loss product or program before you reduce your wallet in an effort to reduce your waistline.

TRUTH

The CIA medical scam

Who could possibly fall for a claim that the CIA has spy satellites that can scan your body—while you sleep—for medical problems undetectable by conventional means, and that once identified, these problems can be cured by secret medicines—also while you sleep—that will keep you in robust health? No one, you say? Wrong. For six years, this story was the one used by Stacey Finley to scam people throughout Louisiana, Texas, and Mississippi out of close to a million dollars.

We often hear only what we want to hear. A quick and easy route to good health is enticing. The federal prosecutors of Stacey Finley described her victims as "solid, middle-class, educated citizens."* These same people trusted someone because they thought they knew her. They thought she was their friend. They wanted to believe. Wanting to believe is a scam artist's greatest ally. The lesson here is not to fall into the herd mentality. Scam artists depend on us following the recommendations and endorsements of well-meaning, trustworthy people, who themselves got taken in by these scams. Scam artists use the naiveté of their victims to expand their influence. There is no substitute for skepticism and doing your own research. Fortunately, there is much legitimate medical information available online. Some valuable sources are the Merck Manuals (www.merck.com/pubs), the National Institutes of Health (www.nih.gov), the U.S. Department of Health and Human Services (www.os.dhhs.gov), and the U.S. Food and Drug Administration (www.fda.gov).

Beware of touted products that will cure just about anything. Don't trust testimonials. Legitimate medicines and treatments don't carry testimonials. Beware of the quick fix. And don't fall prey to the conspiracy theorists who tell you

Legitimate medicines and treatments don't carry testimonials.

they have a secret medicine being suppressed by the large pharmaceutical companies because they will lose their profits if everyone becomes aware of this miracle cure.

* "Woman Pleads Guilty in Bizarre Medical Scam." *Associated Press.* Jan 22, 2007.

TRUTH
23

Education scams

Scholarship scams

Unless you're careful, trying to find the money for higher education can put you at risk of being scammed. You may be encouraged to pay a fee to apply for a scholarship that you never receive. People often think that they merely have not won the scholarship—not that they have been scammed out of their money.

You may apply for an educational loan that carries a particularly low interest rate. However, there is one catch—you have to pay an advance fee to apply for the loan. Unfortunately, you never receive the promised loan, but you do manage to lose your advance fee. Any fees that may be required for a legitimate educational loan are deducted from the money you receive from the lender. You don't have to pay the fees in advance.

Then there is the scholarship that you are notified you have already won, although you never applied for it. Any kind of prize, scholarship, or award that you are told you have won even though you never applied for it is probably a scam.

Some companies promise they'll match you with scholarships that you'll be eligible for, and that if you don't get the scholarship, they'll refund your money. Some of these companies are legitimate. Sort of. They may not be looking to steal your money, but they don't have any greater access to free scholarship information than you do, particularly in these days of the ubiquitous availability of information on the Internet. You can find sources for free scholarship information at www.finaid.org, www.fastweb.monster.com, and www.nasfaa.org, which is operated by the National Association of Student Financial Aid Administrators. Other companies offering to find a scholarship for you merely take your money and vanish into the night. You may be offered a money-back guarantee, but you probably won't get your money back.

Many scholarship scams involve financial aid consulting. Financial aid consultants are not all scammers. Honest financial aid

> Any kind of prize, scholarship, or award that you are told you have won even though you never applied for it is probably a scam.

consultants help people navigate through the Free Application for Federal Student Aid (FAFSA) form for a fee of anywhere from $50 to $100. Others may charge as much as $1,000 to provide unethical information that can get you in trouble. Often these scammers tell you that they can show you how to shift ownership of family assets to increase the chances of getting greater needs-based financial aid. There are no legal tricks or strategies they can provide that you cannot obtain for free by going to www.finaid.org. Also be aware that if you pay a financial aid consultant for services, even if those services do not include assistance in actually filling out the FAFSA form, the consultant is required by law to sign the FAFSA form. If the consultant refuses or is hesitant to sign the form, that should alert you to the possibility that you are dealing with an unethical advisor.

Watch out for anyone offering a scholarship who tells you that they need your credit card or bank account number just for identification purposes to hold the scholarship.

Diploma mills

A college degree can be helpful in getting a better job. But, as always, people look for shortcuts. Attaining a college degree can be a long and arduous process. You actually have to study. But what if you could get a college degree based on all that you have learned in life, your work history, or as the advertisements say, your "life experience?" That is the promise found in the advertisements placed in legitimate publications that tout the ability to get a college degree based not on a rigorous course of study, but rather just upon your accumulated wisdom garnered through years of on-the-job experience or just your "life experience." Sound too good to be true? It is. Phony colleges that sell college degrees without requiring you to do any actual academic work to achieve that degree are called *diploma mills*, and the whole thing is a scam. Having a college degree can be helpful when applying for a job, but having a phony diploma will not enhance your resume. In fact, it can actually hurt your chances for employment if a prospective employer recognizes the degree listed on your resume as one that has been issued by a diploma mill.

So, how do you identify a diploma mill? Diploma mills often have names that appear quite legitimate or similar to institutions that you know are legitimate. Columbia State University is a diploma mill.

Columbia University is an eminent Ivy League school. They have nothing to do with each other, but the similarity in their names can cause confusion.

Use common sense. What's the value of a degree you didn't have to do much academic work for? How significant is a diploma for which you had to do little or nothing more than pay your tuition, which can be as much as $5,000? Scammers exploit the fact that legitimate institutions do, in some instances, grant some credit—and I emphasize only some limited credit—for your work or life experiences. You still must complete substantial academic work to earn a degree. Also making it easier for this scam to appear legitimate is the fact that although many of these diploma mills exist exclusively online, most legitimate educational institutions now offer opportunities to take courses online.

A school that offers you a degree based exclusively on your work or life experience; that doesn't require you to attend actual classes in person or online; that will grant you a degree for the payment of a flat fee as compared to paying for individual courses; and that will guarantee you a degree in a few days or weeks is illegitimate.

If you want to determine whether the school offering a program you're interested in is a legitimate school that's accredited by a legitimate source of accreditation and not by a sham organization that may even be sponsored by the phony school, you can go to the interactive Web site of the U.S. Department of education at www.ope.ed.gov/accreditation to check on the validity of the degree that you're being offered.

A final word to the would-be wise: Not only may you be scammed if you pay for a worthless degree, you may also be committing a crime if you use the degree granted by a diploma mill. Some states, such as Oregon, have criminalized the use of diploma mill degrees by their "graduates."

> Not only may you be scammed if you pay for a worthless degree, you may also be committing a crime if you use the degree granted by a diploma mill.

TRUTH

Romance scams

Online dating scams

The Johnny Lee song, "Looking for Love in All the Wrong Places," featured in the movie *Urban Cowboy* might also be a good name for the various romance and dating scams that may be found on the Internet.

Online dating services and Web sites are in great supply, and many of them are quite legitimate. However, there are some illegitimate ones that are out to steal more than your heart. They also want your money. As in many other Internet scams, Nigeria is prominent in online dating scams. Similar to the Nigerian letter scam, the Nigerian dating scam gains your confidence by allowing you to make contact with someone who, like you, is looking for love. Online correspondence between victims and scammers progresses to a point where love grows and trust is established so that it doesn't seem unreasonable when the object of the victim's online romance asks for help cashing a check from his work in Nigeria or elsewhere. The scammers send checks or money orders to their victims, telling them that they can't cash the checks in Nigeria for various technical or bureaucratic reasons, and ask the victims to cash the check, wire the money, and even keep a portion of the check as a token of their appreciation. Needless to say: The check is worthless. The victim is left with a broken heart and a reduced bank account when the check that appeared to be so legitimate bounces, while the check that the victim sent to her romantic partner in a land far away lessens her own bank account.

> The Nigerian dating scam gains your confidence by allowing you to make contact with someone who, like you, is looking for love.

A picture is worth a thousand words

Online dating services generally include photographs of the participants. Many phony Nigerian dating scams have used pictures of models from the Web site www.focusagencyhawaii.com. Focus Hawaii is a legitimate company, but its pictures have often been misappropriated by scammers.

Russian dating scam

From Russia with Love was the second James Bond movie, but it also could be the name of the scam that hooks people looking for romance on the Internet with allegedly Russian men and women who, after the relationship has sufficiently progressed online, hit their victims up for money to come to the United States or for other seemingly legitimate purposes back in Russia. Many of these scams are part of a highly organized crime ring in the Russian Republic of Mari El, which has been an independent country since 1990. Pictures used are often of Russian celebrities, but they also may be of ordinary, but attractive local women who are paid a small fee for their photographs. The organizers of this scam have rooms full of computers and, in many instances, local students, typing away the correspondence and getting paid a 10 to 15 percent commission on the money they con their victims out of worldwide. Despite the efforts of law enforcement in Mari El, this scam continues.

Secret admirer scam

Having a secret admirer can be flattering. Having a secret admirer steal your computer passwords, credit card numbers, and online banking information can be devastating. This particular scam begins when you receive an email that appears to be from one of the many online greeting card companies. Online greeting cards are a legitimate business. The cards can be clever combinations of music and animation. Not to mention the fact that if you forgot someone's birthday till the birthday itself arrived, you can still send a card that gets there on time. Many of these online greeting card companies offer free cards.

The names of the online greeting card companies are familiar to many people. It's easy as you go through your emails not to notice that what appears to be a notice of a card from one of the legitimate companies is instead from one with a very similar name. So you go to the email that contains a message that you have received an online greeting card with a link to the card. If you go to the link, you see the card sent to you by your secret admirer. Unfortunately, by linking to the malicious Web site, you also have unwittingly downloaded a Trojan horse, keystroke logging program that, without your being aware of it, tracks everything you do on your computer and sends

Unfortunately, by linking to the malicious Web site, you also have unwittingly downloaded a Trojan horse, keystroke logging program.

this information to the identity thief who was your secret admirer. The keystroke logging program passes along your credit card number if you buy anything online as well as other personal information that you may enter into Web sites that you think are secure. In fact, the Web sites you go to may indeed be secure, but your computer is not. It is infected by the Trojan horse, keystroke logging program.

This particular scam is actually easy to avoid. The key to this particular greeting card scam is a chink in the armor of Microsoft's Windows software—a chink that Microsoft fixed with the MS06-014 patch that was released at no cost to Microsoft Windows users in May 2006. Merely by keeping software patches up-to-date when reminded to do so, many victims of this scam might have avoided being scammed.

TRUTH

Rental car insurance

We've all had this happen to us. Pressure to buy rental car insurance.

You rent a car on vacation, and the clerk at the counter goes through some of the terms of the rental agreement with you. It is long, confusing, and full of fine print, much of which remains undiscussed. Standing out in the form, however, is a section that the clerk points out to you and is so significant that it requires your initialing of a special box to indicate your choice. The special box deals with the optional insurance that the car rental agency urges you to purchase. It is at that time that many people have a brain freeze as you try hard to remember what you have heard regarding this insurance. Will your credit card cover your insurance needs? Does your own automobile insurance policy cover the same risks? The cost of the insurance can considerably increase the cost of renting the car, so the stakes are high. Do you need the coverage?

The truth is, in many instances, this is a legal scam. Generally, if you own a car and have your own automobile insurance, its coverage carries over to protect you while driving your rental car when the rental is not for a business trip. In addition, some credit card companies still provide insurance coverage for you while driving a rental car paid for through their credit card. The key to making the right decision and not getting scammed is to check with your automobile insurance agent and your credit card company well *before* your trip to learn precisely what coverage you have and what limitations there may be.

> Generally, if you own a car and have your own automobile insurance, its coverage carries over to protect you while driving your rental car when the rental is not for a business trip.

TRUTH

Personal information privacy

The privacy of your personal financial information held by companies you do business with, such as banks or credit card companies, is not just a matter of these companies sharing this information with other companies who flood you with junk mail solicitations. As we see in the news, businesses are hacked into almost every week by identity thieves who harvest this information and use it to steal your money and ruin your credit. The more places that have your personal financial information, the more likely you are to become a victim of identity theft.

In 1999, Congress passed the Gramm-Leach Bliley Act. Congressional press releases bragged about the protections this new law would bring to consumers concerned about the privacy of their personal data. However, if you actually read the law, you would find that rather than provide substantial consumer protection, the law's primary objective was to permit banks, insurance companies, and investment companies to merge and do business together more effectively.

You probably remember receiving the first annual disclosure of the privacy policies of the financial companies, such as insurance companies, credit card companies, and brokerage companies you do business with, as required by the Gramm-Leach Bliley Act. But then again, maybe you don't remember, because these disclosures just looked like much of the fine-print junk mail that we often get from these companies. Many people didn't even take the time to read these disclosures, and you can't blame them, because the confusing language often baffled those that did take the time to read these disclosures. The privacy disclosure was required by law to be clear, conspicuous, and accurate. Unfortunately, it was anything but clear, conspicuous, and accurate. The disclosure was supposed to inform consumers about the particular company's policy regarding sharing your personal information with other companies.

> The more places that have your personal financial information, the more likely you are to become a victim of identity theft.

Unbeknown to many consumers was the fact that, prior to the enactment of this law, many of the companies that you do business with were providing your personal information, not just to companies that they might have been affiliated with, but even with telemarketers. The law now at least no longer permits the sharing of this information with telemarketers.

Consumers were told by Congress that their right to protect the confidentiality of their personal information was provided for in the law by giving consumers the ability to opt out of permitting the companies that they do business with from sharing that information with other companies. Forgetting for the moment the question as to why we should have to opt *out* of having our personal information shared rather than being required to opt *in* if we wanted our information to be shared with other companies, the truth is, even if you opt out of information sharing, the law is seriously flawed by loopholes and exceptions that still permit information sharing even if you opt out.

Even if you opt out of sharing information, the company you do business with can still share your personal information with any company it's affiliated with. An *affiliated company* is a company that's either owned or controlled by the company you do business with. In addition, even if you opt out of information sharing, the company holding your information can also share your personal information with any company it has a joint marketing agreement with. An example of a joint marketing agreement is where your bank agrees to endorse or offer insurance policies issued by another company.

> Despite what Congress tells you, your ability to require businesses that have your personal financial information to keep that information private and secure is quite incomplete.

So, ultimately, despite what Congress tells you, your ability to require businesses that have your personal financial information to keep that information private and secure is quite incomplete.

Yet, the truth is, if you haven't yet opted out of sharing this information, you should do so when you receive your next annual notice of your right to do so. Although opting out won't totally limit the ability of the companies you do business with from sharing this information with other companies, it's still better than nothing.

TRUTH

Cramming

here are some frauds so well
conducted that it would be stupidity
not to be deceived by them.

—*Charles Caleb Colton*

Cramming is not just for exams. *Cramming* is also the name for unauthorized charges that appear on your telephone bill. These charges may be a one-time rip-off, or they may turn into a regular monthly dip into your wallet. Telephone bills today are so complicated, long, and full of fine print that many people either do not bother to read them, or just give up when they can't understand them. Either way, scammers adding phony charges to your telephone bill rely on your inability to discover that you are a victim of cramming to continue their scam.

As Pogo, the cartoon character of years past, said, "We have met the enemy and he is us." We often cause ourselves to be victimized when we're not particularly careful. Many times at sporting events or other public gatherings, there will be booths sponsoring sweepstakes. It only takes a few moments to fill in a sweepstakes application that carries the potential of a big prize. Unfortunately, few of us take the time to read the small print that provides the details of the sweepstakes. Buried within the fine print of some of these sweepstakes' materials is a notice that informs you that by completing the sweepstakes form, you are also signing up for a telephone calling card or other service that will be added to your telephone bill. Sometimes you don't even get the service, but you always get the bill. In either case, it's a scam to be avoided.

> By completing the sweepstakes form, you are also signing up for a telephone calling card or other service that will be added to your telephone bill.

Some key phrases to look for in your telephone bill to determine if you are being crammed are "Miscellaneous charges and credits," "Min Use Fee," "Activation Fee," "Member Fee," "Voice Mail Fee," or, for that matter, any fee that you don't recognize. If you find such cramming charges, there will be instructions on your telephone bill as to how to dispute them.

TRUTH

28

900 numbers

When you call a telephone number that begins with 900, you're entering the world of telephone pay per call. Originally, 900 numbers were seen as a way for people to receive information or entertainment without having to use a computer. Unfortunately, although legitimate companies use 900 numbers and comply with the laws that regulate them, many unscrupulous scammers use 900 numbers to scam people out of their money.

One scam involves responding to an advertisement for a job by calling an 800 number. People are usually confident that when they call a telephone number that begins with the digits 800 or 888, they're calling a toll-free number. Generally, that's true. However, many people are unaware of a scam through which the 800 number that you call gets transferred to a 900 number and, without your being aware of it, you're charged for the call. In one particular job advertisement 900 number scam, when you call the 800 number, you're greeted by a recorded message that asks you to press #9 to verify your phone number. Unsuspecting victims do so without realizing that by pressing #9, they have just transferred their call to a 900 number. Once this is done, the unwitting victim is asked question after question, not for purposes of an interview relating to a job, but merely to keep the victim on the line so that the phone charges incurred while discussing a nonexistent job can grow and grow. This switching scam is prohibited by federal regulations, but that doesn't stop the scammers from making these calls.

> When you call the 800 number, you're greeted by a recorded message that asks you to press #9 to verify your phone number. ...by pressing #9, they have just transferred their call to a 900 number.

If you're a victim of this switching scam, you will not become aware of being victimized until you see your next telephone bill containing the scam-related charges. Contact your telephone company and tell them to remove the fraudulent charges from your bill. You should, however, be prepared to be harassed by a collection agency on behalf of the scammer even if you are successful in having the charges removed from your telephone bill. If you are contacted by a collection agency attempting to collect on an 800 number call that was switched to a 900 number call, tell the collection agency that you were switched from an 800 number to a 900 number without being told, which violates federal regulations.

TIP You may want to consider having your telephone provider put a block on your telephone line to prevent access to 900 numbers from your telephone number.

The truth is, even some 800 and 888 telephone numbers are permitted to charge you for calls if the call provides audio entertainment or information services. However, the law requires that these companies comply with the FTC rules that regulate 900 numbers. These rules require that you be asked at the start of the call to pay with a credit card or make billing arrangements at that time. The company must also provide you with its name, address, business telephone number, and rates for its services.

Direct American Marketers, Inc. (DAMI) sent out millions of sweepstakes notices throughout the country telling people to call a 900 number to claim the prize they were lucky enough to have won. Unfortunately, the only big winner of this sweepstakes was DAMI. The average 900 number telephone call by "winners" inquiring as to the prize they had won in a contest that they had not entered was about seven minutes, which resulted in a charge of anywhere from $20 to $40 being added to their telephone bill. Following actions by a number of states' Attorneys General, DAMI went out of business and declared bankruptcy.

> Federal law requires sweepstakes promoters to tell you the odds of winning before you have to call a 900 number.

The truth is, federal law requires sweepstakes promoters to tell you the odds of winning before you have to call a 900 number. The promoters are also required to tell you how to get the information as to whether you have won or lost for free. A loophole in this federal law, however, is that this does not apply to contests where you have to answer a question, regardless of how simple, to win. The bottom line is that 900 numbers are moneymakers, but not for the caller.

TRUTH

Phony caller ID

Phony caller ID is a real boon. If you get a call from someone you don't wish to speak to, you merely let your answering machine take the call. If it is someone you do wish to speak to, the caller ID screen tells you who is calling, so you don't have to worry about recognizing her voice.

However, caller ID isn't always accurate. Identity thieves are able to manipulate caller ID systems so that telephone calls from them appear to be from someone else, such as, for instance, the local district court. People who have fallen for a particular variation of this scam received a telephone call that appeared to be from their local district court. When they answered the phone, they were told that they had failed to appear for jury duty. When the victims told the caller that they didn't receive a notice to appear for jury duty, the caller then asked for personal information, such as a Social Security number to confirm the identity of the person receiving the call. Once the victim did that, the trap was sprung. The scammer had all the information needed to make the person receiving the call a victim of identity theft.

You should never give personal information over the telephone to anyone you haven't called, regardless of what your caller ID may say.

You should never give personal information over the telephone to anyone you haven't called, regardless of what your caller ID may say.

TRUTH

Area code 809

Area code 809 is the area code of a telephone number you are asked to call by way of a message left on your answering machine.

Most people are unfamiliar with the 809 area code or think that it, like 800 numbers, represents a toll-free call. The truth is, area code 809 is an area code for much of the Caribbean, most of which, except for the U.S. Virgin Islands and Puerto Rico, are not subject to American laws and regulations that regulate pay for call services. The message that you receive tells you to return the call for any number of compelling reasons, such as that you have won a prize, that a family member is sick or died, or even that a family member has been arrested. If you return the call, you will be charged $25 per minute, and the person on the other end of the call will endeavor to keep you on the phone as long as possible to run up your bill.

You should never return a call from an 809 area code unless you know the person calling, such as a relative vacationing in the Caribbean. If you do fall victim to this scam, you will find a large charge for the call on your next telephone bill. Immediately, you should contact your telephone company and long-distance carrier and inform them that you are disputing the call. Your telephone service cannot be terminated for your refusal to pay for these calls. However, as with scam 900 number calls, you should be prepared to be contacted by a collection agency attempting to collect on the call. Fortunately, even if the call was not subject to federal regulations, the scammer will not be able to collect the "debt" through a foreign court. The scammer must get a judgment against you in the United States, and it is unlikely that the scammer will file a lawsuit against you in an American court, so don't be bullied by a collection agency that threatens to take you to court. In fact, the threat to take you to court to collect the "debt" may even constitute an unfair collection practice in violation of federal law.

> You should never return a call from an 809 area code unless you know the person calling, such as a relative vacationing in the Caribbean.

TRUTH

31

Fear and loathing of the IRS

"By the time the fool
has learned the game, the
players have dispersed."

—*African proverb*

The income tax is fertile ground for scammers. No one likes paying taxes. Unfortunately, the almost universal desire to avoid paying income taxes can be exploited by conmen with phony tax scams. There also are some people who believe that the federal income tax itself is a scam. This belief is also used by con artists to advance their scams. Even our fear of the IRS and our desire to follow the rules when contacted by them can be used against us when it comes to phony tax scams.

The "Slavery Reparations" scam, for instance, continues to be with us despite the best efforts of the federal government to quash it. Conmen tell African Americans that, for a fee, they will help them get a substantial tax credit or refund that the law provides as reparation for slavery. Often the con artists tell their victims that although this is

The almost universal desire to avoid paying income taxes can be exploited by conmen with phony tax scams.

the law, the government is quite secretive about this to reduce the number of people who can take advantage of it. Once again, a kernel of truth is enough for a conman to grow a scam that can entrap people who want to believe. In this case, at the end of the Civil War, Congress passed a bill authorizing the payment to all former slaves of 40 acres of land and a mule as compensation for their enslavement. However, the bill was vetoed by President Andrew Johnson and never became law.

The risks of getting involved in this scam can be significant. You not only lose the money that you pay the con artist, but you also risk being assessed a $500 penalty by the IRS for merely making the claim and thereby filing a fraudulent income tax return. Previously, the IRS did not assess this penalty unless a person had filed a claim for slavery reparations after being informed by the IRS that the claim was invalid. However, now the IRS takes the position that it may assess the penalty against anyone who files such a claim, even once.

The IRS' attempts to quash this scam certainly were not helped by its own admission that it had mistakenly paid out as many as 200 slavery reparations claims for a total of $30 million. However, once these mistaken payments were discovered, the IRS took action to recover the money improperly sent to those people who did receive slavery reparation payments.

You don't even have to leave the comfort of your home to become a victim of a scam. Some conmen come to your door and tell you that they are from the IRS and that they are there to collect your taxes. The truth is, no IRS field auditor would ever come to your home without calling first. He also would have a photo identification card. In any event, if someone comes to your door and tells you that he is from the IRS, you can always call the IRS directly to check on the identity of the person on your stoop.

Phony tax forms

Scammers often use phony tax forms to obtain your personal information, which is used to turn you into a victim of identity theft.

One scam tax form appears to be an official request for information from your bank or the IRS. It requests personal information such as your marital status, place of birth, bank account numbers, employment history, and parents' names. The form looks quite official and, as often is the case, has some similarity to legitimate forms. Another phony form that has been making the rounds is a "Reporting and Withholding Exemption Form" that purports to be from your bank or the IRS. This particular scam form asks for your PIN and the maiden name of your mother. No such IRS form exists. And no IRS form ever asks about your mother or your PIN.

Another commonly used scam tax form is a Form W-9095, which is titled Application for Certificate Status Ownership for Withholding Tax. This form has

> No IRS form ever asks about your mother or your PIN.

a strong resemblance to the legitimate IRS Form W-9 Request for Taxpayer Identification Number and Certification. Anyone who has ever obtained a mortgage loan with a tax escrow account is familiar with the W-9. However, the phony form asks for much more personal identifying information than the W-9.

Whenever you're confronted by a tax form you're unfamiliar with that asks for personal information, check with the IRS to make sure it's not a scam.

TRUTH

32

More tax scams

Notices from the IRS usually are dreaded. They rarely seem to be good news. But, that's not so when you're receiving a tax refund.

One scam that takes advantage of this mindset occurs when you receive an email that claims to be from the IRS. One scammer used taxrefunds@irs.gov as an email address. Another phony address used was admin@irs.gov. Both addresses sure look good, but they sure are bad. In the letter from the phony IRS, you're told that you're eligible for a tax refund. To obtain your tax refund, you're told to use the form that you can access through a link in the email. The link takes you to a phony IRS Web site that asks for personal and financial information. The first thing to remember if you receive such a letter is that the IRS won't notify you by email, and they won't ask for personal identifying information or financial information. You should also keep in mind that it isn't necessary to file a form other than your income tax return to obtain a tax refund. Finally, don't under any circumstances download anything in an email that you think may not be genuine. Unbeknown to you, you may be downloading a keystroke logging program that can infect your computer and transfer all of your computer's activity to the identity thief who sent you the message.

> It isn't necessary to file a form other than your income tax return to obtain a tax refund.

Electronic filing tax scam

Filing your tax return electronically can be quite helpful in avoiding a number of situations in which your income tax return could be misappropriated and used to steal your identity. However, this very system, which is called the Electronic Federal Tax Payment System (EFTPS), is also used as the basis for a scam to steal your identity. The scam starts when you receive an email purportedly from the IRS that tells you that someone else has used your credit card and tried to pay income taxes through the EFTPS. To correct the situation, as well as receive funds that the IRS is holding in the victim's name, you must click on a link in the email to go to an IRS Web site and complete a form. Unsuspecting victims who do go to the Web site find something that looks official, but actually it's not. The Web site asks for personal information such as Social Security number, credit card numbers, passwords, and PINs. If you provide the information, you're sure to become a victim of identity theft.

The Treasury Inspector General for Tax Administration, the federal agency that investigates tax fraud, found numerous phony IRS Web sites emanating from 18 different countries including Argentina, Aruba, Australia, Austria, Canada, Chile, China, England, Germany, Indonesia, Italy, Japan, Korea, Malaysia, Mexico, Poland, Singapore, and Slovakia. No matter how authentic they may look (and it's easy to compose a phony Web site with graphics that look like the legitimate IRS), the IRS doesn't use email to contact people, and the IRS doesn't ask for personal financial information. In addition, look at the Web site's address. It may be a tip-off. One such phony Web site was http://tzk.kozle.pl. Whenever in doubt, call your friends at the IRS directly at 800-829-1040 to find out whether any contact you have received from the IRS is genuine.

> The IRS doesn't use email to contact people, and the IRS doesn't ask for personal financial information.

IRS is illegal scam

No one likes paying income taxes, but they are legal. People who believe scammers who try to sell them a system to avoid having to pay federal income taxes are asking for trouble. The IRS has never lost a single court case on the issue of whether the federal income tax system is constitutional. The arguments used by people selling you their "inside" information as to how you can avoid paying income taxes may sound legitimate. They may even quote statutes and regulations that you're unfamiliar with, that really sound compelling, but the bottom line is that all of these schemes share one basic element—they're scams.

TRUTH

33

It just doesn't stop

Phony trusts

Phony trusts that sometimes go under the name "Pure Trusts," "Pure Equity Trusts," or "Common Law Trusts" are another scam tactic that the promoters of these trusts know is not a legitimate way to avoid taxes. Placing all your assets in a trust that you control doesn't avoid income taxes. However, this fact doesn't stop the promoters of such trusts, used for income tax avoidance, from selling the scammer's "special knowledge" and such trusts to avoid paying income taxes.

David Marvin Swanson's business, Dynamic Monetary Strategies, sold fraudulent trusts that he called unincorporated business trust organizations which, according to Swanson, could protect income and assets from federal income tax. The federal government disagreed and obtained an injunction preventing him from making these representations and selling these trusts. Since 2001, more than 200 similar injunctions have been obtained, shutting down phony income tax avoidance schemes.

> Placing all your assets in a trust that you control doesn't avoid income taxes.

Offshore accounts

Another scam used by people to avoid income taxes is putting assets in an offshore bank account. Indicative of the fact that offshore accounts are subject to federal income taxes is the section on your IRS 1040 form where you are required to answer, under the pains and penalties of perjury, questions as to whether you have any offshore bank accounts or trusts. People with offshore accounts are faced with the choice of lying to the IRS and committing perjury or telling the truth and alerting the IRS to a possible scam. Thinking that they are more shrewd than Wile E. Coyote, some promoters of these offshore scams have promoted offshore accounts in various Caribbean countries that have strong financial privacy laws figuring what the IRS doesn't know can't hurt them. The fatal flaw in this plan, however, is that although people access their money in these accounts through credit cards issued through these foreign banks, the records for

American Express, MasterCard, and Visa for operations in the Caribbean are headquartered in the United States, where the financial privacy laws of these countries such as the Cayman Islands, Antigua, Barbados, and the Bahamas do not apply. So much for Wile E. Coyote, super genius.

IRS collections

A letter from the IRS is not one of life's pleasures. A call from a collection agency is also not something that people tend to enjoy. Put them together, and you have a gift to conmen and identity thieves. The IRS, in its infinite wisdom, has started a program through which thousands of taxpayers who owe less than $25,000 may be contacted by private collection firms that have been hired by the IRS to collect overdue taxes, penalties, and interest. The IRS is hiring private collection agencies to collect this money even though the cost to the government of having these overdue taxes collected by collection agencies is much higher than having IRS employees do it. But that isn't the worst of the situation. The possibility of fraud by people claiming to be from a private collection agency authorized by the IRS to collect taxes is great. The truth is, the simplest way to protect yourself from potential fraud is to just not deal with these collection agencies at all. If you're contacted by someone purporting to be from an IRS authorized collection agency, you have the right to merely respond that you will only deal with

> Section on your IRS 1040 form is where you are required to answer, under the pains and penalties of perjury, questions as to whether you have any offshore bank accounts or trusts.

> If indeed your overdue tax bill has been turned over by the IRS to a private collection agency, you will receive a letter informing you of this fact before you ever hear from a collection agency.

the IRS directly. You should also be aware that if indeed your overdue tax bill has been turned over by the IRS to a private collection agency, you will receive a letter informing you of this fact before you ever hear from a collection agency. If you do decide to work with a collection agency that tells you it is collecting overdue taxes on behalf of the IRS, you should never make your check payable to anyone other than the U.S. Treasury, and your check should only be mailed to an IRS address that you have confirmed is legitimate.

TRUTH

34

Social Security

t's morally wrong to allow
a sucker to keep his money.

—*W.C. Fields*

Confusion about government benefit programs is fertile ground for scammers. Social Security has been the basis for many con artists, who use this confusion to take advantage of unwary seniors.

One common Social Security scam involves promises by the criminals that they can get back to you from the federal government all of the Social Security tax payments you've made throughout your lifetime. For the proverbial "small fee," which is usually about $100 and a percentage of the refund that never comes, the con artist promises to file the proper claims forms with the IRS. The truth is, there's no such program. Social Security tax payments are never refundable. The victims pay their fees and wait for a refund that never comes.

> Confusion about government benefit programs is fertile ground for scammers.

Direct deposit verification scam

Another Social Security scam involves a call you receive from someone purporting to be from the Social Security Administration who says that he needs to verify your direct deposit banking information. It's easy to fall victim to this type of scam, but the truth is, you should never give personal information over the phone to anyone whom you haven't called. If you think that a call from Social Security might be legitimate, you should call your local Social Security Administration office to confirm the identity of the person calling you.

The windfall scam

Yet another Social Security scam occurs when you're told that your benefits are being reduced because you've inherited a home or money from a deceased relative. You're told that you must pay back benefits you've received. The truth is, Social Security isn't a program based on need or that you must qualify for by having a limited amount of assets, so the basic premise is wrong. Yet, unwitting victims pay the amounts demanded to the scammers, who say they're collecting on behalf of the government.

One particularly insidious Social Security scam preys on our fear of identity theft. Many people have received an email that purported to be from the Social Security Administration warning the recipient that they were the victim of identity theft and that someone was using their Social Security number. They were then directed to a phony Web site that looked like an official Social Security Administration Web site, where they were directed to confirm their identity not just with their Social Security number, but also bank information, credit card information, and even PIN information. This is the real indicator that you're being scammed. The truth is, under no circumstance would the Social Security Administration ever ask for your credit card information and certainly not your PIN. Once again, the rule is that you should never give out personal information to someone that you didn't contact, and only then when you're confident that the information being given is secure. When in doubt, call Social Security if you ever receive anything that says it is an official communication seeking personal information.

> When in doubt, call Social Security if you ever receive anything that says it is an official communication seeking personal information.

COLAS

Colas can be quite refreshing. For Social Security recipients, *COLAs*, which is an acronym for Cost of Living Adjustments, are annual additions to Social Security benefit checks that get paid automatically to recipients. Each year, scammers take advantage of news stories about COLAs to scam people through identity theft. Typically, the Social Security recipient will receive an email, such as was done in a large-scale scam in late 2006, that there will be a cost-of-living adjustment beginning in January of the next year. However, then comes the hook and the scam. The email goes on to tell you that, to receive your increase in benefits, you must update your personal information with the Social Security Administration. And even worse, you're told that if you don't update your information by a

Ask yourself: Why would the Social Security Administration ever have to ask for your Social Security number?

specified date, your benefits will be suspended. However, you're also told that you can merely click on a link to the Social Security Web site to update your information and ensure that you'll continue to receive your benefits and get the scheduled cost-of-living adjustment. This is a scam. It's a phishing expedition. The link you're directed to takes you to a Web site that looks like the genuine Social Security Administration Web site, but it's a phony one that asks for personal information, such as your Social Security number, that's used to make you a victim of identity theft. The truth is, you should never provide your Social Security number to anyone online unless you're absolutely sure about the identity of the person you share it with. As for this particular scam, you might also ask yourself: Why would the Social Security Administration ever have to ask for your Social Security number?

TRUTH

Medicare

Medicare, the national health insurance program for people over the age of 65, is an attractive area for scams. Like most medical insurance programs, it's complicated, and this always feeds into the hands of scammers. In addition, many older Americans are more trusting than many younger people, which also makes them attractive targets. Finally, Medicare is an insurance program that involves the deep pockets of both insurance companies and the U.S. Treasury, which makes the stakes high for scammers looking for a lucrative target.

Medicare prescription drug scam

The recently enacted Medicare prescription drug program is helping millions of American seniors pay for their prescription drugs. But it's confusing. As always, scammers take advantage of this confusion to their own ends. Many seniors have received telephone calls about a phony prescription drug plan being offered as a part of the Medicare Part D prescription drug program.

> Medicare is an attractive area for scams. Like most medical insurance programs, it's complicated, and this always feeds into the hands of scammers.

The scam has become known as the "299 dollar ring" because that's the typical amount that a Medicare-eligible senior is told to withdraw from his checking account to enroll in the fictional plan. Other times, the caller asks for your checking account information, credit card information, or other personal information that can be used to steal money from you. The answer to these calls should always be the same. As Nancy Reagan used to say, "Just say no." No legitimate Medicare prescription drug plan has an initial enrollment fee. And no legitimate Medicare prescription drug program will ever ask you for personal information over the phone.

TRUTH

36

Veteran scams

Veteran's insurance scam

No one is safe from being targeted by scammers, and veterans of the military service are no exception. Additionally, veterans are accepting of the fact that much of the way that our government in general and the military specifically operate is filled with complexity, which makes the job of a scammer that much easier.

Many veterans have been receiving notices that appear to be from the Veteran's Administration informing them of recent federal legislation that provides for a "dividend" on the life insurance that all military personnel are provided while they are on active duty. Notices of this new law have also even been posted on bulletin boards in VA medical facilities. According to the email, letter, or notice, the new law provides for a payment of as much as $528 to insured veterans. The notice also states that veterans are eligible for this benefit even if they didn't maintain their insurance after leaving the service. Then comes the kicker. The veteran is informed that the benefit is not automatic. He's told that he must apply for the benefit and must provide identifying information, such as birth date and Social Security number.

This is another identity theft scam. There's no such law. Scammers merely use the personal identification information provided by victims of the scams to steal their identity. The best course of action, as always, when asked for personal information by anyone whom you haven't contacted directly is to contact the legitimate organization at a telephone number that you know is correct and verify the accuracy of the original communication.

> Contact the legitimate organization at a telephone number that you know is correct and verify the accuracy of the original communication.

Veteran's Administration pharmacy

Disabled veterans are another easy target for scammers. A recent scam involved disabled veterans receiving a telephone call from someone representing himself to be from the VA pharmacy, saying that they needed personal information, including the veteran's Social Security number along with a list of the prescription drugs he is taking, because of new co-pay regulations. In some instances, the caller tells the veteran to supply a credit card number to pay for such co-payments.

This is a scam. The information taken is used for identity theft and to make charges to the victim's credit card. There are no such new regulations pertaining to co-payments for veterans who use the Veteran's Administration to obtain their prescription drugs, and under no circumstances does the Veterans Administration contact veterans by telephone for personal information or regarding prescription renewals. The rule to follow, as always, is not to give out personal information on the phone to anyone unless you're positive as to the identity of the person requesting the information.

Medicare free medical equipment scam

There are no free lunches, and there certainly are no free motorized wheelchairs. A common Medicare scam occurs when a scammer offers medical equipment or medical screening tests to a Medicare recipient. Your new friend may tell you that even though the particular piece of medical equipment or test is not generally covered by Medicare, he knows how to manipulate the system to get Medicare to cover the expense. The truth is, before Medicare will pay for medical equipment, a doctor must certify that the equipment or test is medically necessary. Some scammers fake signatures or use crooked doctors as accomplices to file false claims. In both cases, you're in danger of getting a bill for equipment that Medicare refuses to pay.

> Before Medicare will pay for medical equipment, a doctor must certify that the equipment or test is medically necessary.

In other instances, scammers troll for seniors on the telephone, in malls, or in retirement homes with offers for medical services that will be paid for by Medicare. You provide your Medicare number, but you get nothing in return except a bill to your insurance company.

The truth is, you should never give your Medicare number to any company that says it provides medical services unless the service has been coordinated with your primary care physician.

TRUTH

Credit cards

*ho is going to believe a con
artist? Everyone, if she's good.*

— Andy Griffith as Matlock

It isn't uncommon for you to receive a notice for a credit card that seems to say that you've been preapproved (whatever that may mean) for a credit card that may provide you with a low interest rate, a high credit limit, and an incredible rewards program. In fact, it may promise just about anything. The truth is, the preapproval letter actually is just an invitation to apply for a credit card at an interest rate that will be determined later depending on your credit report and credit history.

When you actually receive a credit card after responding to the "preapproved" application, you should make it a point to carefully read the fine print of the card holder agreement, not just the letter that comes with the card, because within the tiny print and the confusing language of the card holder agreement is found the actual terms of that particular credit card. You may find that the terms bear little resemblance to what you thought you were getting.

> The preapproval letter actually is just an invitation to apply for a credit card at an interest rate that will be determined later depending on your credit report and credit history.

Unfortunately, the law still permits credit card companies to mislead people, particularly people who do not take the time to read the fine print. Failure to read the fine print in a credit card agreement can be detrimental to your financial well-being. Cigarette packages carry warnings. Credit cards probably should, too. It isn't unusual for people to seek a new credit card with a high enough credit line to carry the balance transferred from a previous card as well as carry new purchase debt. However, sometimes people assume that they've gotten the credit line they applied for and use their new card for the first time only to find out that the entire credit line was used by the transferred balances, leaving them with an over-the-credit-line fee and a card that has no credit left for purchases. If you find that the terms of the credit card you receive are not what you thought you were getting, don't activate the card. Cut it up. Or call the credit card company and try to negotiate the terms you want. If you can't get those terms, be prepared to walk away. Don't just not use the card. Don't even activate it, because merely activating the card may subject you to fees and adversely affect your credit report.

TIP If you don't want to receive unsolicited credit card offers, you can opt out of receiving the so-called preapproved credit card solicitations by calling 1-888-5-OPT-OUT or by going to the Web site of the consumer credit reporting industry, www. optoutprescreen.com. Some of you may be a bit wary when you call the telephone number or go online to have your name deleted from the lists, because you're asked for your Social Security number, but you can feel relatively confident that this is not a scam. Far from being a scam, having your name taken off these lists can dramatically improve your chances of not becoming a victim of identity theft.

Credit card fees

Fees are big business for credit card issuers. Go over your credit limit by the slightest amount, and you may be facing a penalty fee. To make matters worse, this penalty fee can be assessed on your account multiple times during the same month because many banks impose this charge whenever a charge is over your credit limit rather than at the end of the month. And, to add insult to injury, banks may approve a charge at the time it is made even though it puts the customer over his credit limit and then hit the customer with a penalty fee. The credit card issuers say that they allow you to exceed your credit limit as a "convenience" to you. And, to make things even worse, the fine print in your credit card agreement may permit the credit card issuer to raise your interest rate to a figure higher than the drinking age if you go over your spending limit.

And even if you're completely up-to-date in your payments at all times, and even if you have a "fixed" rate credit card, the credit card company can change your interest rate whenever it desires by giving you 15 days notice of the change. A fixed rate merely means that, unlike a variable rate that automatically increases in accordance with a regular index, your fixed rate is fixed for only as long as the credit card issuer desires and can change whenever the issuer of the credit card so determines.

Universal default

You make sure you pay your credit card bill every month on time. Surely you're at no risk of having your credit card interest rate singled out for a large penalty-triggered increase. After all, you didn't miss a payment, and you weren't late with a payment. Unfortunately, you're still at risk. The fine print in some credit card agreements says that

Always read the fine print.

if you're late with any payment to anyone—the telephone company, your car payment, or your rent, for example—the credit card company reserves the right to increase your interest rate to a punitive rate as high as 32 percent. Always read the fine print.

Late fees scam

If you read your monthly credit card statement carefully, you will note that your monthly payment must not only arrive by a specific day, but by a specific time within that day, such as 1:00 p.m., or your payment is considered late and you are subject to a punitive late fee. These late fees add up. Between 1995 and 2006, according to the General Accountability Office, late fees rose more than 160 percent, to an average of $33.64. About 70 percent of the more than $17 billion that the credit card issuers assessed in penalty fees in 2006 came from late fees.

A particularly irritating variation on the late fee is the Same Day Payment Fee, where your credit card issuer charges you a fee, usually about $15, for transferring money electronically from your bank to the credit card issuer. In other words, if you find that your payment has not been made in a timely fashion, leaving no time to send it through the mail, and you send it in electronically to avoid a late charge, you're charged an "on time charge" merely because you sent the money electronically.

TRUTH

38

More credit card offers

Credit card balance transfers

Many banks encourage you to transfer your outstanding balances from other credit cards to a new credit card that they issue you. By doing this, you're promised that you'll be able to pay off your outstanding credit card balance at a low or even zero percent interest rate.

But if the bank issuing the new credit card is charging you no interest on the amount you're transferring, they must be looking to make a profit on your business somewhere else. Generally, if the bank is offering you a zero percent interest rate on the balance of your previous credit card that you're transferring to the new credit card, they will be charging you a profit-making interest on new purchases you make using the new credit card. And in another example of there rarely being anything fine in fine print, the conditions of your new credit card will generally state that any payments you make will be first applied to the transferred balance, with interest accumulating on any and all purchases made using the new credit card. In addition, although you may get a low percent interest rate by transferring an outstanding balance to a new card, there are, of course, charges for transferring the balance. At one time, the fee was 3 percent of the amount that you transferred, with a cap of generally $75. However, now many credit card issuers have lifted the cap, so a transfer of a balance of $7,500, for example, may cost you $225 even though that amount bears no relationship to either the cost or the risk of transferring the balance to the new card.

> They will be charging you a profit-making interest on new purchases you make using the new credit card.

The check is in the mail—convenience checks

All of us who have credit cards periodically receive from our friends at the credit card company a block of "convenience checks" that we can use to access the credit line of our credit card. Convenient they may be, but they also could be considered a legal scam. Start off with the fee for using the convenience check that may be 3 to 4 percent of the amount of the check. Add to this the fact that the interest rate for these convenience checks is probably greater than the voting age. And then comes the risk from the illegal scammers. If the blank convenience checks are stolen from your mail and used by an identity thief, you won't know about it until you read your next credit card monthly bill and see the shocking news. Unlike unauthorized charges on a credit card, where your liability is limited by federal law to no more than $50, there is no federal law that limits your liability with convenience checks. And although you can stop credit card companies from sending you solicitations for new credit cards, you cannot stop them from sending you convenience checks. You can ask very nicely, but the credit card companies don't have to honor your request.

Credit card theft insurance

The credit card companies are excellent at selling you things you don't need. If they could, they would sell umbrellas in the Sahara desert. So it should come as no surprise that they sell you insurance to cover your losses if your card is stolen or lost. But why would you even consider paying for this when your maximum exposure if your card is lost or stolen is only $50, and most credit card companies don't even charge you that amount?

Credit card disability insurance

Disability insurance may be one of the least used and most important insurance coverage available today. However, even Thomas Jefferson would have to admit that not all disability insurance is created equal. As always, it's important to read the fine print. The limited disability insurance offered to you by your credit card company may defer your monthly payments, but it

The limited disability insurance offered to you by your credit card company may defer your monthly payments, but it doesn't reduce or forgive any amounts owed that continue to accrue compound interest while you're disabled.

doesn't reduce or forgive any amounts owed that continue to accrue compound interest while you're disabled. In addition, under the terms of such insurance, you can't even use your credit card during this period of disability. The truth is, what you're getting doesn't seem to be worth the price, and if not an illegal scam, it sure walks like a scam and quacks like a scam.

TRUTH

39

Skimmers and ATM scams

Skimmers

Skim milk may help to keep you thin, but a skimmer may make your wallet thinner.

A *skimmer* is a small electronic device about the size of a deck of cards that is used by a rogue salesclerk, waiter, or anyone to whom you give your credit card to steal from you. This person swipes your card through the skimmer, which reads the information contained on the magnetic strip on the card and gets all your personal information contained on the card. Identity thieves then use this information to fraudulently use your credit card and steal your identity. In many instances, the people initially skimming your card gather the information contained on the skimmer about your card and many others victimized at the same location and sell this information to other criminals, who use the information to create phony credit cards. And just like the cost of so much technological equipment such as flat screen televisions have come down over the years, so has the cost to criminals of skimming equipment. Skimmers can be bought over the Internet for a few hundred dollars, and the equipment to make counterfeit credit cards with the information gathered on the skimmer can be had online for a few thousand dollars.

A good practice is to watch your credit card from the time it leaves your hand until the time you get it back. Unfortunately, this is not always an easy rule to follow, particularly in restaurants.

> A good practice is to watch your credit card from the time it leaves your hand until the time you get it back.

Fraud scams

Federal law limits your liability for the fraudulent use of your credit card if it's lost or stolen to $50. And, in most instances, the credit card companies even waive this charge. However, often the greatest harm that occurs when you become a victim of identity theft is not the money that you lose directly through the misuse of your credit card and your identity, but rather the damage that occurs to your credit report, where unauthorized charges may appear and affect your ability to obtain credit in the future. To protect your credit report, it's critical that you monitor your monthly credit card statement carefully for unauthorized charges. The sooner you notice a problem, the easier it will be to put a stop to the crime and fix your credit.

When you use a debit card, you're even more vulnerable than when you use a credit card.

When you use a debit card, you're even more vulnerable than when you use a credit card. Although a debit card looks like a regular credit card issued by MasterCard or Visa, it provides immediate access to your checking account. In addition, federal law does not provide the same $50 limit for unauthorized charges. If you're not careful, you can have your entire checking account emptied without legal recourse if you're tardy in reporting the misuse of your debit card.

Having your card skimmed at an ATM can lead to a fraud that skims more than the surface of your bank account. ATMs are a wonderful, modern convenience that we've all grown dependent on. Using an ATM is a quick and easy way to access your bank account for some quick cash. Unfortunately, using an ATM can also be a quick and easy way for scammers to steal your money right out of your account by using a skimmer and a camera. A small skimmer is attached by the scammer to the ATM where you insert your card. The skimmer then reads the information on your card as you insert it into the ATM. Meanwhile, a camera—which may even appear to be a security camera—installed at the location of the ATM looks over your shoulder and observes your PIN as you enter it into the ATM.

Armed with the information gathered from the skimmer and the camera, the thieves can create a duplicate card with your information and use it along with your PIN to access the money in your account.

The truth is, to avoid being victimized by this scam, you should always carefully observe any ATM you use for evidence of tampering or anything else that appears unusual in the machine itself, particularly in the card-insert area. And always shield the keyboard as you enter your PIN.

Always shield the keyboard as you enter your PIN.

The Lebanese Loop

Another ATM scam is commonly known as the Lebanese Loop. The way this scam works is that when the victim inserts his card into the ATM, it fails to register when he enters his PIN. After repeatedly and unsuccessfully inserting his PIN, the victim usually leaves, assuming that the machine has swallowed the ATM card, which the machine didn't return after being inserted.

Sometimes there's a sign on the ATM informing the victim that it's necessary to enter your PIN three times; other times there may be a "helpful" stranger nearby who says that he had the same problem with this machine not registering his PIN until he entered it three times. Many victims are quite willing to accept the help of this good Samaritan and follow his advice, but they're disappointed when the ATM still doesn't permit their account to be reached, nor does the machine return the card.

The truth is, a scammer has previously altered the particular ATM machine by inserting into the card slot a thin plastic sleeve that disables the ATM from being able to read your card when you put it into the ATM. There's nothing particularly magical or significant about the number of times that you enter your PIN. What is significant is that by entering your PIN multiple times, it gives the scammer standing by you at the ATM multiple times to "shoulder surf" and note your PIN as you repeatedly try to access your account. Once you've given up and left the ATM, the thief pulls out the plastic sleeve and, now armed with both your ATM card and your PIN, can get into your account and steal your money.

So, what can you do to protect yourself from this type of scam? Always make sure that no one (or no well-positioned camera) can observe your PIN as you enter it. Also, you should be wary of any signs around the ATM that provide instructions for use of the machine that appear to be out of the ordinary. You also might want to get into the habit of carefully inspecting the card insert mechanism whenever you insert your card to make sure that it hasn't been tampered with, either by a Lebanese Loop or a skimmer.

One more thing. If you ever *do* have your card eaten by an ATM machine and not returned to you, you may receive a telephone call purportedly from the police or bank security telling you that they've recovered your card but need your PIN for confirmation purposes. Don't give the caller that information. The call is not from the police or bank security. The call is from a scammer who wasn't quick enough to get your PIN when you were originally scammed and is now using this new tactic to get your PIN that will provide him with access to your account.

Get into the habit of carefully inspecting the card insert mechanism whenever you insert your card to make sure that it hasn't been tampered with.

TRUTH

40

Free credit report

Everyone can obtain a copy of their credit report free once a year from each of the three major credit-reporting agencies: Equifax, Experian, and TransUnion. You can order your free credit reports online at *https://www. annualcreditreport.com or* by phone at 1-877-322-8228. You can also mail an Annual Credit Report Request Form, which you may obtain at the FTC's Web site of *www.ftc.gov,* to Annual Credit Report Request Service, P.O. Box 105281, Atlanta, Georgia 30348-5281.

Making sure your credit report is accurate is important for many reasons, but it's particularly helpful to alert you if you have become a victim of identity theft. Many people don't learn that they've become a victim of identity theft until they check their credit report and see accounts that they never authorized that are either outstanding or in collection.

As always, be alert; there are a number of companies with names and Web sites that are similar to the official Web site that you may obtain your free credit reports from but that will charge you for their services after a free trial period ends. Some of these Web sites have names that contain common misspellings or typographical errors that might easily be typed by someone seeking the real free credit report Web site. If you sign up for a "free" credit report through any of these services, you may also be obligating yourself to

> **Many people don't learn that they've become a victim of identity theft until they check their credit report and see accounts that they never authorized that are either outstanding or in collection.**

additional services that you may not need or want to buy. Often these involve getting your initial credit report free, but unwittingly signing up for a continuing costly credit monitoring service. Buried in the fine print are the dirty details as to additional services that you may be obligating yourself to if you sign up with one of these "free" services. A typical scam provides your free credit report with an additional 30 days of free credit monitoring; however, unless you have the eyes of an eagle, you may miss the fine print that tells you that unless you notify the company promptly within those 30 days that you wish to cancel the contract for future credit monitoring services, you're hooked into a long-term contract that is anything but free. Unfortunately, as misleading as the tactics of these companies might be, technically they may be acting legally.

Credit monitoring services are of dubious value in any event. Prior to authorizing a major purchase on credit, a merchant will check the purchaser's credit report to ensure that the person is creditworthy. Even if an identity thief obtained your Social Security number or other important identifying information, if your credit report was kept secure by the credit reporting agencies so that access to the report was only permitted when you, and not an identity thief, had authorized access, the effects of the identity theft could be greatly reduced. However, rather than meet their responsibility to keep this information secure, the major credit reporting agencies offer to sell you credit monitoring services and notify you of any unusual or suspicious activity. The problem with this approach is that the credit reporting agencies inform you of a problem *after* the problem has occurred rather than help *prevent* the problem. It is as if you were hit by a truck while crossing the street and someone came over to you while you were lying in the highway to tell you that you had just been hit by a truck. I would much rather have someone warn me before the truck hit me. If credit reporting agencies instituted better security policies and supported universal credit freeze legislation, there would be less unauthorized access to our credit reports. The truth is, the actions and inaction of the major credit reporting agencies contribute to a problem for you, which they, for a fee, then offer to help solve by providing you with credit monitoring services of questionable value.

TIP When a credit reporting agency signs you up for this "free" credit report, it may tell you that it needs your credit card number merely to establish your account or verify who you are. The truth is, the purpose of getting your credit card number is solely to charge you for future services as soon as the initial 30-day period has ended. A good piece of advice is never to use your credit card to pay for something that is supposed to be free.

I advise people interested in getting their free credit report to go to the FTC Web site (www.ftc.gov) and click on the link to a free credit report to make sure you're going to the truly free official Web site.

Many people who have taken to heart my message about not providing personal identification information except in the most limited of circumstances are concerned when they are required to provide personal information including their Social Security number and birth date to get free credit reports. However, with the major warning that you must be sure that you're giving this information to the proper entity to obtain your free credit reports, this information is needed to obtain your free credit report, and you shouldn't be worried that this is a scam.

TIP Although you may obtain a free copy of your credit report from each of the three major credit reporting agencies once each 12 months, you don't need to do them all at the same time. A good habit to get into is to request your credit report from one of the credit reporting agencies and then four months later request one from another credit reporting agency and eight months later request one from the last remaining credit reporting agency so that you're reviewing your credit reports every four months for free.

Free credit reports and identity theft

Another scam occurs when criminals lure you to a Web site that appears to offer access to your free credit report but instead takes the identifying information you provide under the guise of assisting you in obtaining your free credit report and uses it to steal your identity.

So how can you tell if you're being scammed by an offer of a free credit report? First, check for misspellings and poor grammar in the email message from anyone soliciting you to obtain a free credit report through their services. It's been said that no generalization is worth a damn—including this one—but it does quite often appear that criminals don't proofread their copy and don't pay particular attention to their grammar. The connection between criminals and bad grammar may not be definitive, but it does appear to be real. Perhaps junior high school English teachers are in some way responsible for the crime wave of today.

Another simple test to see if the Web site you're using to obtain your free credit report is legitimate is to go to www.networksolutions. com and click on the "WHOIS" search, which indicates who actually is operating the particular Web site.

TIP Never use a Web site that asks for personal information that has no relation to confirming your identity. No one needs to know your PIN or credit card numbers to authenticate who you are for purposes of providing you with a free credit report.

Finally, a way to make sure that you're on a secure site is to look for the padlock icon at the bottom of your computer screen. Also look for an s on the Web address following http so it reads https, which indicates that the data is encrypted and the site is secure.

TRUTH

41

Credit repair services

Vulnerable people who have gotten in over their heads in debt often find themselves desperate for a way out. Being in debt is a three-headed monster, because not only are you hounded by your creditors, but in addition, heavy unpaid debts will negatively affect the credit score contained in your credit report which, in turn, will have a negative effect on your ability to get a job, buy insurance, rent an apartment, buy a car, or get a mortgage. In their desperation, many people turn to fraudulent credit repair services that promise to solve all their problems. Unfortunately, all they may find is a scam that takes their money.

The advertisements for credit repair services are pervasive and persuasive. You find them in legitimate newspapers and magazines, on television, on the radio, and all over the Internet. Unfortunately, many of the credit repair services you read and hear about are scams. We should know better. Some make elaborate claims that sound too good to be true because they are just that. They promise to erase your bad credit instantly, create a new clean identity for you instantly, and remove bankruptcies as well as other bad credit information from your credit report. These are just a few of the false claims made by unscrupulous credit repair services to lure you to them.

The law mandates that adverse credit information remain on your credit report for seven years, except for bankruptcies, which are permitted to remain on your credit report for ten years. Credit repair services run by con artists will tell you that they can get rid of negative information on your credit report and give you a clean record. Legally they cannot. Verifiably correct information cannot be removed from your credit report until the applicable seven- or ten-year period has elapsed.

Verifiably correct information cannot be removed from your credit report until the applicable seven- or ten-year period has elapsed.

Clifton Cross double-crossed his customers through his credit repair company, Build-It-Fast, which promised to erase bad credit and obtain a new clean credit report for its customers. Cross used a common illegal technique called file segregation. Customers were told how to obtain an Employer Identification Number from the IRS by filing a form SS-4 and then use the number to set up a new credit history for themselves and thereby abandon and segregate their bad credit history. IRS form SS-4 is properly used to get a taxpayer identification number for an employer, a trust, an estate, or other legitimate business. This number has the same number of digits as a Social Security number. Through file segregation and using the new identification number in the place of their Social Security number, Cross' customers attempted to establish clean credit reports and isolate their bad credit.

The truth is, file segregation is illegal. Hiding a true credit history is illegal. Anyone who tells you that she can remove accurate

Hiding a true credit history is illegal.

information from your credit report earlier than seven years from the time of the reported financial transaction is lying to you, stealing your money, or inducing you to participate in a crime. Clifton Cross was sentenced to 49 months in federal prison for his illegal activities.

TRUTH

42

Credit counseling agencies

Legitimate credit counseling agencies can be a boon to people with debt or credit problems. Among their most important services, they provide financial education programs to help you identify the behavior that may have resulted in your debt problems. In many circumstances, they can negotiate a plan with your creditors through which your creditors may agree to accept reduced payments, reduced finance charges, or even waived late fees. Many times they will require you to pay a single payment each month to the credit counseling agency, which will then, in turn, pay your creditors the agreed-upon amounts as part of a comprehensive debt repayment plan.

Such plans often take from one to four years to liquidate your debts. Many credit counseling agencies charge little or nothing for their services, while others charge small monthly maintenance fees. If this sounds too good to be true, you are right to be skeptical. However, many credit-counseling agencies are actually partially funded by payments from the credit card companies and other creditors. These payments from the credit card companies and other creditors are called fair share payments and represent a classic example of a win-win solution. Through such a plan, the creditors can help support an industry (the credit counseling agencies) that helps the credit card companies

> Such plans often take from one to four years to liquidate your debts.

receive a larger portion of their outstanding credit card debt than if the consumers went bankrupt or if the debts became uncollectible while, at the same time, reducing the amount of the debt that the consumer has to pay. Originally, the fair share payments to the credit counseling agencies averaged between 12 and 15 percent for managing a debt management plan; however, in recent years, these payments have been reduced to an average of 6 percent.

Unfortunately, giving an industry that does good work a bad name are a large number of scam credit counseling agencies that hide behind tax-exempt status and have little interest in helping you fix your credit but are quite interested in getting some of your money while your debt and credit problems continue to grow.

So how do you tell the good guys from the bad guys in this industry? If an agency wants a large initial payment before it does anything for you, that is your signal to walk out the door. Federal law mandates that you are not required to pay a credit repair service until its work has been completed.

If an agency suggests that you apply for an Employer Identification Number to establish a new clean credit history, just say no. That is the first step in file segregation, and it's illegal.

If your first payment goes to the credit-counseling agency instead of your creditors, this is a good sign that it's a bad company.

> If an agency wants a large initial payment before it does anything for you, that is your signal to walk out the door.

Finally, if the agency's solution for everyone is a consolidation loan, beware. Credit counseling scams often involve being referred to another company they control that will lend you money to consolidate your debts when such a loan is unwarranted.

How to pick a credit counseling agency

- Comparison shop. Smokey Robinson was right: "You better shop around."

- Check out a few agencies and don't provide any personal financial information before you determine which agency you wish to use.

- Only consider credit-counseling agencies that are affiliated with the National Foundation for Credit Counseling (NFCC) or the Association of Independent Consumer Credit Counseling Agencies (AICCCA). These are legitimate companies that adhere to ethical standards.

- Investigate whether the company you're considering has any complaints against it with your state's Attorney General's consumer protection division as well as the Federal Trade Commission.

- Don't pick a credit-counseling agency that can be found only in the phone book or on the Internet. Go to its office.

- Find out the range of services the agency provides and make sure it includes financial counseling and not just the establishment of a debt management plan.

- Make sure you understand the costs as well as any and all fees involved.

- Make sure that the agency won't share your personal information with any other entity without your approval.

TRUTH

43

Credit card rate reduction scam

Would you be enticed by a telephone call purportedly from someone connected to your credit card company telling you that he could help you reduce the interest rate on your credit card to as low as 4.75 percent? Many people are.

And why not? If you have caller ID, the call appears to be from your credit card company. The cost for this service is generally hundreds of dollars that, you are told, will be totally refunded if the promised credit card interest rate reductions are not obtained. So what is there to lose? Upon sending the company the initial money, you receive a form to fill out that requests information about your credit cards and other debts as well as requesting your Social Security number and other identifying personal information.

Once the scammer receives the information, minimal services are provided to the extent of a three-way telephone conference call with you, the scammer, and your credit card company, during which a lowered interest rate is requested. Although this request generally is denied, you don't receive the promised refunds of the fees you paid for this service.

The particular scam I am describing originated in Canada and was shut down by the FTC. The scammer used technology that permitted it to have its initial calls to its victims appear to be coming from the victim's credit card company. This is called *caller ID spoofing*, and it's a reason that you can't trust your caller ID to be a totally effective fraud screener. Although credit card companies have the ability to reduce credit card rates for individual cardholders, it's an ability that they rarely exercise, and only then in unusually compelling circumstances. You should always be wary of anyone who promises that he can get your credit card interest rate lowered. If you receive a cold call from someone saying that he is affiliated with your credit card company offering assistance in lowering your credit card interest rate, you should dismiss the call out of hand. Credit card companies don't operate in this fashion. If you want to check into it further, you can contact your credit card company's customer service people at the genuine telephone number found on your monthly statement.

TRUTH

44

Advance fee credit cards

Getting by in our society without a credit card is difficult. Have you ever tried to pay for a rental car or make a hotel reservation without one? But getting a credit card may be difficult for people who have a bad credit history or a bankruptcy.

Preying upon people who are desperate to get a credit card are scammers who place advertisements in legitimate newspapers and send out mass mailings offering credit cards with credit limits of as much as $7,500 regardless of your credit history. All you need to do is pay a processing fee, which may be anywhere from $50 to $90. The names of the companies offering these credit cards sound like companies you're familiar with, but having a name that sounds legitimate is just part of the scam. Legitimate credit card companies don't charge you a processing fee for a credit card under any circumstances until you're actually approved for the particular card. In fact, what you may receive from the scammer for your processing fee is no credit card at all, but merely a list of banks that offer credit cards. None of these banks have any relation with the scammer. The payment that you made to the scammer does not in the slightest way make it any more likely that any of these banks will offer you a credit card. But that is not even the worst of it. Other conmen working a variation of this same scam merely take your money for the processing fee and send you nothing at all. And, worst of all, you become a potential victim of identity theft by providing your personal information to the scammer.

> **Legitimate credit card companies don't charge you a processing fee for a credit card under any circumstances until you're actually approved for the particular card.**

Another form of advance fee credit card fraud occurs when people are scammed into believing that they are being sold a regular credit card, but find out that what they are actually sold is a credit card whose use is limited to purchasing merchandise contained in catalogues issued by the same company selling you the card. The cost of the credit card is usually a couple of hundred dollars. And, to make matters worse, often the products that you can buy through the catalogue are more expensive than you would be charged if you bought the items elsewhere. Compounding the fraud even further are the fees you're charged for this worthless credit card. The initial activation fee is just the beginning of the fees you pay. People buying these cards, which appear to be no-interest credit cards with credit limits of up to $8,000, soon find that in addition to the initial "activation fee," they're charged a host of other fees automatically unless they cancel the card immediately.

The scammers who sell these cards represent that they help you to establish a credit history that will be reported to the credit reporting agencies and assist you in improving your all-important credit score maintained by the credit reporting bureaus that can affect whether you get a job, insurance, an apartment, or a loan. The truth is, there are much less costly ways to improve your credit score without using an advance fee "credit" card. Moreover, many of the purchases made through the card are not even reported to all of the credit bureaus.

Advance fee credit cards are a sucker bet. You are better off obtaining a secured credit card if your credit makes it difficult to obtain a conventional credit card. A secured credit card is one issued by a legitimate bank—even if you have bad credit—if you establish a bank account that will serve as collateral for your credit card purchases. Through the responsible use of a secured credit card, you can establish your credit until your credit score is sufficient to enable you to obtain a conventional unsecured credit card. It's important to be a prudent consumer when applying for a secured credit card. The fees can vary greatly from bank to bank. If you're a member of a credit union, you might get a secured credit card there at a reduced cost. For a list of banks that offer secured credit cards and the fees that they charge, go to www.bankrate.com.

> Advance fee credit cards are a sucker bet. You are better off obtaining a secured credit card if your credit makes it difficult to obtain a conventional credit card.

TRUTH

Radio frequency cards

"Instant gratification takes too long" was a great line uttered by Meryl Streep in the 1990 movie *Postcards from the Edge*.

Apparently, the credit card companies have adopted this as their motto. It just takes so damn long to process a credit card purchase. And then there is that interminable time it takes to sign a credit card slip. So, utilizing the latest technology, they have come up with credit cards embedded with radio-frequency tags. Now all you have to do is merely wave your credit card in front of a scanner. No swiping your credit card through a machine, no signature, no muss, no fuss. And no security. That's because identity thieves, also using the latest technology, can take the information off of your radio frequency credit card with their own scanner and start charging things in your name. The credit card companies will tell you that the information on your card is encrypted so that someone without the proper decoding device cannot lift it. They also will tell you that you can keep your credit card in a safe holder that will block access to the information on your card. But are the milliseconds saved really worth the added risk to your security?

> Identity thieves, also using the latest technology, can take the information off of your radio frequency credit card with their own scanner and start charging things in your name.

TRUTH

46

Work-at-home schemes

hey were a people so primitive they did not know how to get money, except by working for it.

—Joseph Addison

Like many cons, this one appeals to us on many levels. You get to work at home. Your commute is from your bedroom to your computer. The work is easy. It requires no skill. Your time is your own and, best of all, you make lots of money. All you need to do is get "the word" from the promoter of the scam.

One of the most common types of these is a "work-at-home" scheme where you merely stuff envelopes. And just what are you stuffing into those envelopes? The truth is, often you're sending out information on the same work-at-home envelope stuffing business that you're doing. There's no money in stuffing envelopes at home. The only money made in envelope stuffing is by the scammers who con you out of your money and lure you into this scam.

> There's no money in stuffing envelopes at home. The only money made in envelope stuffing is by the scammers who con you out of your money.

Work at home—medical billing

We all know how complex the health care system is in this country. Advertisements in legitimate newspapers and magazines tell you that medical billing by physicians is a huge business and that little of it is done electronically. In fact, the medical industry is lagging behind much of the business world in its use of electronic billing and information transmittal. It seems reasonable when we're told that with so much money involved in processing medical bills and insurance bills, there's money to be made by enterprising people. We're then told that many physicians don't want to spend their time or their staff's time doing this important billing task. We're told that they wish to send out this work to others to do for them. And that's where you come in. Armed with the proper software, some instruction, and a list of interested physician-prospects, you're promised by the scammer that you'll rapidly be in a position to make large amounts of money doing medical billing and administrative services in the medical field. The cost of this package to put you in business can range from a few hundred dollars to a few thousand dollars, but the results are the same. It's a scam.

This scam is operated by many different people and continues to flourish despite convictions for fraud such as those of the people involved in such a scam under the names Data Medical Capital, Data-Jed, and Medco.

The truth is, the medical billing business is a complex, competitive one that's difficult to get into, particularly without experience. Medical billing involves extensive knowledge of the ever-changing code system used by insurers to designate various procedures. The training you receive from the scammers is worthless. The software program you receive is marked up in price tremendously from what it would cost you to buy the same software at any computer store, and it may not even be the software you need. As to the list of physicians just waiting for you to call, the list is just a compilation of names of physicians, none of whom are likely to be interested in your services.

The advertisements for these scams appear in many legitimate sources, but don't take the fact that such an advertisement appears in a newspaper or magazine that you trust as an endorsement of that particular publication. The truth is, it's not.

> Advertisements for these scams appear in many legitimate sources, but don't take the fact that such an advertisement appears in a newspaper or magazine that you trust as an endorsement of that particular publication.

TRUTH

47

Easy money

What could be easier? Get paid for giving your opinion? Get paid to shop? Get paid for going to dinner at great restaurants? Unfortunately, it's not quite what it appears.

Although there are legitimate companies that will pay people to perform market surveys, the pay is hardly great for the time involved, and the work is far from steady. Scammers count on your willingness to be conned and tell you that by signing up for their program, you will be paid considerable money for giving your opinion of the retail experience at a particular store, eating at a particular restaurant or, without having to even leave your home, just taking a survey. However, what you end up doing when you join these programs is paying more for your membership than you will ever earn. Or worse. These companies might also be planting viruses on your computer, stealing money from your credit card, or making you susceptible to identity theft.

Another variation on the mystery shopper scam occurs when you receive a letter informing you that you've been chosen as a mystery shopper to do product and marketing research for companies you're familiar with, such as Wal-Mart or McDonalds. When you join the program, you're sent a cashier's check for thousands of dollars and instructed to make purchases with the money and evaluate the products. You even get to keep the products. What a deal! However, the check is always for more than the amount of your purchases, so after your fee is taken out, you're instructed to wire the balance of the money by Western Union back to the mystery shopping company. By now, you should have guessed that the cashier's check is as phony as a crocodile's smile. You end up wiring your own money to the scammer without any effective legal recourse to get it back.

> Wiring money is a quick way to empty your account without the legal protections that come with paying by a check that you could stop payment on.

Anytime you're asked to wire money, a bell should go off in your mind, because wiring money is a quick way to empty your account without the legal protections that come with paying by a check that you could stop payment on.

TRUTH

48

More wrong turns

Check cashing scam

You made the mistake of answering an enticing email that tells you how you can make money quickly and easily. Now you're in the business of transferring funds internationally.

How this works is money is sent to you by check, wire transfers, or even certified checks. You, in turn, are told to deposit the money in your account and then send the money back to the person you're dealing with, while keeping a small percentage of the money for yourself. What could be easier? But why do they need you? You're told that your role is important to avoid various international fees and taxes. So you deposit the money in your account and send back the money minus your commission. It's only later that you learn that the check deposited in your account bounces, and you're on the hook for the money you paid back. Think about it. Why would anyone pick an international business partner through random emails? Don't get conned looking for the fast, easy buck.

> Think about it. Why would anyone pick an international business partner through random emails?

Disgruntled postal workers

We've all heard stories of disgruntled postal workers who have responded to problems at work by "going postal," a term not particularly endearing to officials of the United States Postal Service. But why don't we hear more about all the "gruntled" postal workers? Apparently there are many of these contented workers, because their jobs seem to be in such great demand. Jobs with the United States Postal Service are in such demand that scammers see this as an opportunity to separate people from their money regardless of rain, snow, or gloom of night.

Victims of one scam responded to advertisements informing them that the United States Postal Service was hiring for great jobs with terrific benefits. When interested applicants responded by calling the telephone number contained in the advertisement, they were told that there were jobs available in their area of the country, but they would need to pass an examination that would guarantee them a job. The company placing the advertisement told them that, for a fee, they would help them register for a job opening with the postal service as well as provide them with material that would enable them to get a score of at least 90

The score that the applicant gets on the legitimate examination is only one factor in determining whether an applicant gets the job.

on the examination, which would ensure them a job with the post office. Sounds good. Too bad it wasn't true. Like many scams, there is just a kernel of truth to this one. It's true that examinations are required for many entry-level positions with the United States Postal Service. However, the tests are not offered every year. It's also true that if an applicant achieves a score of at least 70 on the exam, he's placed on a register for when postal jobs do become available. When a job becomes available, the local post office looks to the register for that particular geographic location and interviews the top three applicants. However, the truth is, the score that the applicant gets on the legitimate examination is only one factor in determining whether an applicant gets the job. And the exam itself is an aptitude test. It's not the kind of test in which you stand a good chance of improving your score through any kind of study.

TRUTH

49

Cruise ship employment scam

> What could be better than working on a cruise ship, spending your winters in the Caribbean and your summers in Alaska? What's not to love?

This promise has been enticing to many people who have responded to advertisements in legitimate newspapers looking for people to work on a cruise ship. When you respond to the advertisement by telephone, you get to do your interview online. The job is described to you in great detail, as is the pay and benefits package. It looks like a great deal. You just need to send the agency your Social Security number and $150 to cover the cost of your uniform.

The truth is, the whole thing is a scam. And not only have you lost $150 or whatever the scammer charged you for uniforms, an application fee, or a security investigation charge, but you're also in serious danger of becoming a victim of identity theft because you've provided your Social Security number as well as perhaps other personal identifying information.

The first warning should go off in your mind whenever an advance payment is required before you start work for a company. Advance payments are extremely unusual for legitimate companies and par for the course with scammers. Never wire money to anyone whom you're not absolutely positive is legitimate. Once you've wired money, it's gone. If you later find out the whole thing was a scam, you've lost the money. If you believe that the cruise job or other dream job may be something you want to pursue, check out the specific company with the Better Business Bureau, the Federal Trade Commission, and your state's Attorney General's office to make sure that the company is indeed legitimate. Even then, call them back at a telephone number that you know is an actual number for the legitimate company they purport to be to confirm that the offer is legitimate. And remember, just because you see such a job listed in a reputable newspaper or other legitimate media source doesn't mean that the advertisement is legitimate. Little, if any, screening is done by the media of advertisements to weed out the frauds and cons.

TRUTH

Get a job online scams

The convenience of posting a resume online with an online employment service is tremendous. In addition to the convenience, you get the advantage of having your resume available to a large number of prospective employers. Unfortunately, your resume may also be available to a large number of scammers.

A common scam occurs when someone posing as a job recruiter for a legitimate company contacts you. He tells you that he's impressed with your resume, but that before the company can schedule an interview with you, it needs to do a background check on you. To do that, it needs some personal identifying information from you, including your Social Security number.

Your Social Security number is the key to identity theft in the hands of a scammer. You should never provide your Social Security number or other sensitive information to a recruiter or employer until you've met with him in person at his office during normal working hours. Personally meeting someone in this way can help you confirm that she works for a legitimate company. You can also check out the legitimacy of a prospective employer through the Better Business Bureau.

Never provide information in an online resume that can be manipulated into identity theft.

> Never provide information in an online resume that can be manipulated into identity theft.

Don't list your Social Security number, your birth date, your home address, or your telephone number. Even as to your name, it's prudent to use only your first initial and your last name.

TRUTH

51

Home sweet scam

If stupidity got us into this mess, then why can't it get us out?

—Will Rogers

For many people, the biggest investment they will ever make during their lifetime is the purchase of a home. Because real estate is so valuable, it is a prime target for scammers.

One scam involves your being approached by a person who tells you that although he's a reputable real estate investor, he can't get conventional financing from local banks because banks are too conservative in their underwriting standards and they consider him to have too many loans in place even though he's a successful businessman operating a profitable business. But he has a win-win solution to his problem—one that will help him and help you at the same time. He will use your good name and credit to buy a piece of property. You get a couple of thousand dollars merely for letting him use your name to buy the property and obtain a mortgage. You have nothing to lose because he will pay all of the closing costs as well as find a tenant to pay the cost of the mortgage and other carrying costs. He also tells you that after about a year, he will "flip" the property and sell it for a tidy profit that he will share with you. Sounds good? It isn't.

The truth is, although in some instances these straw buyers who lent their name and credit to such transactions actually did get paid, in many instances, the people who provided their name and credit ended up in foreclosure and even personal bankruptcy as the banks came after the straw buyers, not just for the property, but also for any amounts left owing the bank after a foreclosure auction of the property. Often the mortgage amounts were particularly large because the scammer provided illegitimate, inflated appraisals of the properties to get more money out of the scam. Elderly people on fixed incomes but with a lifetime of good credit have been prime targets for this kind of fraud.

Everyone should avoid deals like this. Again, Mom was right. Don't take candy from strangers. No matter how sweet the deal sounds, you're safer avoiding real estate transactions unless you're a real estate professional. Never falsify documents, and never go into business with someone that you don't know extremely well. If you even consider such a proposition, check out the banking references of the person offering the deal to you. Get his credit report. Check local courts for lawsuits. Check with the consumer protection division of your state's Attorney General's office for complaints as well.

> No matter how sweet the deal sounds, you're safer avoiding real estate transactions unless you're a real estate professional.

I'll huff and I'll puff and I'll blow your house down

He wasn't called the big, bad wolf for nothing. Scammers are out there who can do more damage to your home and your finances than the big, bad wolf could ever do. A scam that often preys in particular on elderly homeowners involves the scammer obtaining information from public records as to who owns homes with no mortgages left on them. Often this is an elderly homeowner whose home not only is mortgage-free, but whose home also may have substantially appreciated in value since the homeowner first bought the home. It's relatively easy for a scammer to forge your signature on a deed to himself and then forge a notarization of your signature. There's no regulation that requires anyone to provide evidence that he's indeed a notary public before obtaining a notary seal. Once the title appears to be in the scammer's name, he can then get a large amount of money through a mortgage loan secured by your home and never make a single mortgage payment. Fortunately, your home can't be taken away from you by a forged deed, and you won't owe money on a loan taken out by the scammer, but you're in trouble anyway because you'll be compelled to expend considerable time, effort, and legal fees to clear the title to your home, fix the damage to your credit, and prove the true state of affairs.

Once the title appears to be in the scammer's name, he can then get a large amount of money through a mortgage loan secured by your home.

The truth is, scammers exploit a flaw in the system. Registries of deeds don't require much in the way of evidence as to the identity of the person filing a deed. More registries of deeds should follow the lead of Los Angeles and Philadelphia, where the local Registries inform property owners through the mail when important documents affecting their property are filed.

TRUTH

Variations on a theme

Foreclosure fraud

Financial vulnerability makes people more susceptible to being defrauded. In the wild, predators seek out the weakest and most vulnerable animals for the kill; so do the predators in the "civilized" world.

Mortgage foreclosures are increasing throughout the country. Many people took out adjustable rate mortgages and home equity loans when interest rates were low and property prices high, thinking the bubble would never burst. But it always does. So now that prices in many places have flattened or even gone down and interest rates have increased, many homeowners are facing foreclosure as they find themselves unable to make their mortgage payments. These are desperate times for these people and unfortunately, many of them consider that desperate times call for desperate measures. This may mean becoming more susceptible to the claims of scam artists who tell these people what they want to hear, namely that the scam artist will come to their rescue by taking over their mortgage and paying their loan for them while renting their property.

The truth is, scammers know that it can take as long as a year from the time that a mortgage first is in arrears and a foreclosure proceeding is begun before the home is actually auctioned off. This gives the scammer ample time to rent the house and pocket the rent without paying the bank anything.

Be wary of anyone who approaches you about helping you when you're in dire straights. Too often they are the wolves at the door. Work with a lawyer, a reputable real estate agent, and your banker as soon as you encounter financial difficulties with

> Scammers know that it can take as long as a year from the time that a mortgage first is in arrears and a foreclosure proceeding is begun before the home is actually auctioned off. This gives the scammer ample time to rent the house and pocket the rent without paying the bank anything.

mortgage payments to explore legitimate options to solve your financial problems.

It's never over till it's over

Regardless of how wealthy you are or how smart you may think you are, you can easily become a victim of real estate fraud. One particular scam involves a wealthy buyer who is so thrilled with your expensive home that he gives you a full-price offer and provides a certified check for the deposit that may run into the hundreds of thousands of dollars. But after a couple of days, the prospective buyer decides that he doesn't want the home and, in accordance with the terms of the Offer to Purchase, withdraws the offer and requests that you wire his deposit money back to him. So you do, and the cashier's check that he gave you turns out to be phony, and you're out all of the money that you wired to the scammer.

You should never return money for anything that you're in the process of selling until the check to you has actually cleared. Just because it looks like a cashier's check or bank check doesn't make it one.

Reverse mortgages

A reverse mortgage is the name for a loan that uses your home as security for a loan, just like a conventional mortgage arrangement that we're all familiar with. However, unlike a conventional mortgage, with a reverse mortgage you generally don't have to pay back the loan for as long as you live in the home. This allows people to take the equity out of their home and turn it into cash to meet their daily needs without having to be concerned about making monthly payments. Repayment of the loan with interest is generally done when the borrower sells the home, moves out of the home, or dies, whichever first occurs. For many house-rich, but cash-poor seniors, this might seem to be a great solution to their financial concerns. There are many different types of reverse mortgages and a large number of fees involved in obtaining a reverse mortgage. A reverse mortgage is an expensive way to borrow money. However, it can be particularly expensive if you are conned out of money in the process of obtaining a reverse mortgage.

Taking advantage of the public's interest in reverse mortgages coupled with the public's lack of knowledge about reverse mortgages, scammers have "counseled" people interested in reverse mortgages by providing them with information about reverse mortgages and where they may obtain one. For this information and "counseling," often provided under the guise of estate planning services, they charge unwary seniors a fee of between 6 and 10 percent of the money ultimately borrowed through a reverse mortgage. Once the unwary elderly homeowner has signed up with the scammer, the homeowner gets little in return for the money he pays the scammer. Many times the scammer merely provides the homeowner with the name of a financial institution that deals in reverse mortgages. Sometimes the scammer accompanies the homeowner to a counseling session with a HUD-approved counseling agency that is required as a condition of obtaining a HUD-approved reverse mortgage. HUD has issued a directive to reverse mortgage lenders to stop doing business with these scammers. The information provided by the scammer for which a senior may pay thousands of dollars is available absolutely free from the Department of Housing and Urban Development at www.hud.gov. Reverse mortgages are both expensive and exceedingly complex. If you're considering a reverse mortgage, you should hire a real estate lawyer to help you understand the process and help you determine what's best for you.

The information provided by the scammer for which a senior may pay thousands of dollars is available absolutely free from the Department of Housing and Urban Development at www.hud.gov.

TRUTH

Stock scams

ducation is when you read the fine print. Experience is what you get if you don't.

—Pete Seeger

Pump and dump

We've all received emails that contained glowing recommendations of a particular stock, or perhaps you've learned on an Internet forum about a particular "steal" of a stock that's about to take off. Or maybe you even received an email intended for someone else giving you "inside" information about a particular small company stock that is about to rocket to high profits on the stock market. Just ask Martha Stewart. It's not a good thing.

When you get this email or pick up this information, it looks so harmless and appears to be such an easy way to make a big buck that the temptation may be great. The companies involved in this scam are actual companies, but with such small capitalization that they aren't even required to file reports with the Securities and Exchange Commission, so it's difficult to find good information you can rely on to check out the validity of the tip you receive. If you fall for this scam, you buy the stock, and the stock price soars quickly but plummets just as quickly. The truth is, the original tip you received was sent to a large number of people merely to inflate the value of the stock by creating a demand. As soon as the suckers have momentarily shot the price of the stock up, the scammers dump the stock they bought when it was cheap and vanish with their profits while you're left with a worthless stock and a lesson in greed.

> The original tip you received was sent to a large number of people merely to inflate the value of the stock by creating a demand.

Churning

Churning is the name given to the practice by unethical stockbrokers of making excessive trades of stocks for accounts that they manage on behalf of investors. The reason behind these excessive trades is not to maximize your profits as an investor, but rather to generate more fees for the broker, who gets a commission every time a sale occurs in your account. For this reason, it rarely makes sense to give your stockbroker the authority to trade whenever he wants. And shouldn't you be aware of all the trading that does go on in your account?

All too often, people who are baffled by the stock market and the world of investments blindly place their trust in a broker and get burned by having their accounts churned. These same people often don't read or even open their monthly statements from the broker that would show that their accounts are being turned over frequently because they consider the monthly statements too complicated. They're afraid that they wouldn't understand the statements. Unfortunately, what you don't know can hurt you. Read your monthly statement, and if you notice trades that you didn't authorize or even just an unusually high level of activity in your account, ask your broker for an explanation.

The reason behind these excessive trades is not to maximize your profits as an investor, but rather to generate more fees for the broker, who gets a commission every time a sale occurs in your account.

TRUTH

More investment scams

Promissory notes

Corporations legitimately issue promissory notes as a way to raise money to operate their businesses. Through a promissory note, a corporation borrows money from the purchaser of the note and agrees to pay interest on the money borrowed. The loans are paid back over a period of months or even years.

Even legitimate promissory notes are far from a sure thing. If the company borrowing the money comes upon hard times, the lender may not be paid. In any event, genuine corporate promissory notes are rarely available to anyone other than large corporate lenders and sophisticated, experienced investors. But this doesn't stop scammers from marketing to the general public promissory notes issued by companies that are either not well known or, in some instances, don't even exist. The promise is that you can get as much as a 15 percent monthly return on the money you lend these companies. Many times the promissory notes come with a worthless guarantee or representations that they are secured loans, which they aren't. The promissory notes are sold by sales people, who are often insurance agents, as being a safe investment. Often the insurance agents themselves are not aware that this is a scam, but they too may be blinded by their own greed and the high commissions paid by the promoter of the scam. All too often, the only thing you can safely count on is that you will lose money when the company fails to pay you back the money loaned through the promissory note.

All too often, the only thing you can safely count on is that you will lose money when the company fails to pay you back the money loaned through the promissory note. Promissory notes should be avoided as an investment by individual investors.

Promissory notes should be avoided as an investment by individual investors. If you're still considering investing in promissory notes, you should take the following steps:

1. Check the SEC's EDGAR database to see if the promissory note is properly registered by going to the Web site of the SEC at www.sec.gov.
2. Check with your own state's securities regulator to see if the promissory note is registered.
3. Check with the Better Business Bureau where the company issuing the notes is said to be headquartered for any complaints against the company and to see if it is legitimate.

Prime bank schemes

In this scam, investors are promised huge returns on their investments by being let in on the "secret" investments used by some of the wealthiest people in the world, namely access to the investment portfolios of the world's most elite or prime banks. The only problem is that there are no such investments.

A step up from the smaller fraud of promissory notes is the more complex fraud perpetrated by scammers selling prime bank financial instruments. Like promissory notes, however, these investments promise big returns that never materialize. At the essence of the prime bank instrument scam is the claim that you'll be able to invest in a secret investment program of international banks. The investments appear to be legitimate investments with some of the top banks in the world. Some of the names used for the investments are High Yield Investment Programs, Medium Term

> Investors are promised huge returns on their investments by being let in on the "secret" investments used by some of the wealthiest people in the world...The only problem is that there are no such investments.

Bank Notes, Standby Letters of Credit, Bank Guarantees, or Offshore Trading Programs.

You may even be told, to enhance the apparent legitimacy of the investment, that these financial instruments are issued by, guaranteed by, or endorsed by the World Bank. Another clever ploy used by the scammers selling these "investments" is that you're told that the entire transaction must be kept secret; therefore, no references may be supplied to you. You're told that indeed these Prime Bank investments are the best-kept secret in the world of international banking. Also, you're told that the major banks in the world have been involved in these complicated trading programs among themselves since the creation of the World Bank and the International Monetary Fund. You may be told that only select banks and a few privileged investors are permitted access to these investment programs. In fact, you're required to officially participate in this cloak of secrecy by signing a nondisclosure agreement. You're even told with a wink that this program is so secret that federal regulatory agencies will deny its existence. This certainly helps the scammer when it comes to perpetrating a fraud. Lucky you to be able to join the elite group of people invited to participate in this investment. Sometimes to make the fraud seem more legitimate and appeal to you on yet another level, the scammers tell you that the funds invested are used by these major international banks for various humanitarian purposes, and that indeed, you must agree to have a portion of your exorbitant profits be used for whatever particular humanitarian purpose the scammer tells you is the basis for the particular investment program.

As with so many scams that offer you a special, insider deal, you should ask yourself, why are they offering it to me?

The truth is, there are no such investment programs. They're a total scam. A tip-off is the fact that, unlike any other investment, you won't be able to find any independent information about the investment that you're asked to put your money into. As with so many scams that offer you a special, insider deal, you should ask yourself, why are they offering it to me?

TRUTH

Unusual investment
opportunities

Viatical companies

A viatical settlement company buys life insurance policies from policyholders while the policyholder is still living. The company then makes itself the beneficiary of the policy and continues to pay the premiums. The viatical settlement company makes a lump-sum payment to the original policyholder, who can use the money for long-term care needs, medical needs, or whatever he wants.

The development of the viatical settlement industry was spurred on by the AIDS epidemic, when sick people sold their policies to investors for money to use while they were still alive. Viatical settlements offer a legitimate source of funds for someone with a hefty life insurance policy in force, but with few other assets to meet his needs while alive. Unfortunately, the viatical settlement industry is not well regulated, with only about half of the states regulating these companies. The crux of the regulation problem seems to be a technical one as to whether the companies should be regulated as insurance or investments.

Some scammers hold "free" seminars at which potential investors are told how they can invest in viatical settlement companies. The appeal is that the money invested will go to help a sick person in dire need of cash. It truly appears to be a chance to do well while doing good. Unfortunately, some of these companies, such as Mutual Benefits Corp., which was closed by the SEC for fraud, make false promises of guaranteed payoffs or even sell the same life insurance policy multiple times. The truth is, if people had done their homework before investing with Mutual Benefits Corp., they would have found numerous fraud and criminal charges against

> Viatical settlements remain a viable option in some limited circumstances if you need the money and have a life insurance policy to sell. But as an investment, you should avoid them. The possibility of being scammed is just too great.

the company's principals. Viatical settlements remain a viable option in some limited circumstances if you need the money and have a life insurance policy to sell. But as an investment, you should avoid them. The possibility of being scammed is just too great.

Currency trading

One of the first rules of investing is to only invest in things you know and understand. But what fun or profit is there in that? And who has time to actually learn about something before you invest? Unfortunately, people seem to prefer to invest in things that they don't understand but that promise great profits, which just makes the scammer's job that much easier.

Currency trading is legal. It's also complicated. People who watch media coverage in television sound bites of the world of investment and finance are bombarded by information about the fluctuations in the value of the dollar against the Yen and other world currencies. Some knowledgeable investors, mostly institutional investors, do make money in currency trading by, in effect, betting on which currencies are going up in value and which are going down. It's a risky high-stakes game.

But the exotic lure of getting in on some of this "easy money" with the promise of extraordinary high returns and low risk is too much for many people. They are given sales pitches at "free" seminars. They receive a telemarketing call. They receive emails or snail mail. The scammers who deal in this form of investment fraud are slick and persuasive. A recent hook for scammers involved in currency trading has been the war in Iraq. They use compelling advertising that claims that people "in the know" are making big profits by buying and selling Iraqi currency.

This is a risky investment with rapid price swings that can wipe out profits quickly even when it's done legally. But when you're investing through a scammer who may be operating the scam as a Ponzi deal and has little intent of doing anything other than stealing your money, your chances of coming out of this with a penny in your pocket are slight.

Compounding the problem is that this form of investment is not well regulated even when it's done legally. Currency trading can be a form of a futures contract, which is an agreement to buy or sell a commodity on a specific date in the future. As such, it's regulated by the Commodity Futures Trading Commission, a federal agency. However, loopholes in the law legally permit some futures contracts to be classified not as futures contracts and, therefore, aren't subject to federal regulation.

If you're considering investing in currency trading, you should first investigate the people with whom you're considering investing with your state's securities commissioner. You can find out who that is in your state through the Web site of the North American Securities Administrators Association, an organization made up of all of the state securities regulators. That Web site can be found at www.nasaa.org/home/index.cfm. You should also check with your state Attorney General and the Commodity Futures Trading Commission at its Web site of www.cftc.gov.

> You should first investigate the people with whom you're considering investing with your state's securities commissioner.

TRUTH

Fees in legitimate investments

Variable annuities

Variable annuities are a technically legal investment that can easily morph into a scam. In fact, the North American Securities Administrators Association has called variable annuities one of the top ten scams of the year because of the failure of many salespeople to tell their customers of the extensive fees and charges they involve. Unscrupulous salespeople love variable annuities because the commissions are as high as 12 percent, but unwary customers, including many older people who are particularly unsuited for this investment, have come to hate them. Variable annuities are touted as being able to bring a greater investment return than other investments, but as a general rule with most investments that make that promise, they come with more risk.

A *variable annuity* is a tax-deferred investment that has an insurance component and subaccounts made up of various mutual funds. It's done as a contract with an insurance company that promises to provide regular payments to you in the future. The size of the payments depends on the performance of the mutual funds that make up the investment portion of the variable annuity. As with any investment, it's not the money you make that's important, but rather the money you keep. With a variable annuity, the money you get to keep is drastically reduced by the many fees involved. The fees found in a typical variable annuity can be quite high, particularly as they compound over time.

> Variable annuities are one of the top ten scams of the year because of the failure of many salespeople to tell their customers of the extensive fees and charges they involve.

The Mortality and Expense Risk Charge is an annual charge that is usually about 1.25 percent of the value of the account. This charge relates to the insurance aspect of your annuity.

The Account Maintenance Fee is a fixed fee of about $35 per year that compensates the insurance company issuing the annuity for administration costs. However, in addition to this fee, you will indirectly pay the management fees of the various mutual funds that make up the investments contained in your annuity.

Then there are the surrender fees. Not since the days of General George Armstrong Custer have there been stiffer surrender fees. Depending on the individual annuity, taking your money out of a deferred variable annuity to invest in something else or merely to use the money can carry a surrender charge of as much as 7 percent of the value of the annuity. Surrender charges can exist for as long as ten years in some deferred variable annuities. These surrender charges make deferred annuities a particularly poor investment choice for many older Americans who may have a need to readily access their funds but who are often a target audience of sellers of variable annuities.

Sellers of variable annuities tell customers that there are income tax advantages to owning a variable annuity because the income you derive is tax deferred, like a traditional IRA. What they don't tell you is that when you take money out of your variable annuity, it's taxed at higher ordinary income tax rates rather than the lower capital gains income tax rates you would be paying for a comparable investment in a mutual fund. If you owned the same mutual fund both inside an annuity and outside an annuity, you would pay income taxes at the lower capital gains rates when you took the money out of your individually owned mutual fund, but you'd pay at the higher ordinary income tax rates when you took the money out of your annuity.

The truth is, most people would do considerably better by investing their money directly in the various mutual funds that make up the subaccounts of the annuity with fewer costs.

> Most people would do considerably better by investing their money directly in the various mutual funds that make up the subaccounts of the annuity with fewer costs.

Mutual fund fees

Mutual funds are not only legal, but they can also be a simple way to get a ready-made diversified investment portfolio. However, the level of fees found in some mutual funds can turn a legal investment into a legal scam.

All mutual funds must disclose their fees and charges in their prospectuses. The prospectus must also contain a chart that shows the effect of the particular fund's fees and charges on a $1,000 investment over one-, three-, five-, and ten-year periods. Unfortunately, most people don't bother to read the prospectus. You should.

Some of the fees and charges that you may find in a mutual fund include front-end load fees, redemption fees, management fees, and marketing fees.

> Most people don't bother to read the prospectus. You should.

Front-end load fees are sales fees on mutual funds sold through a broker or financial planner. Often the fact that this fee is present is not readily discerned unless you read the prospectus. Load funds don't earn more money than no-load funds that don't charge you a sales commission, so unless you need the help of a broker or financial planner to choose a fund for you, you're wasting your money buying a load fund.

Redemption fees are just back-end loads. They represent a fee you pay merely for the privilege of selling your shares in the mutual fund. Again, unless you read the prospectus, you may not be aware of this fee that can eat into your profits.

Management fees are necessary, but they can range considerably from one mutual fund to another from .5 percent to 1.0 percent annually. In addition to this fee are charges for administrative costs of the fund that range from .2 percent annually to .4 percent.

But the biggest legal scam fee of all is the *Mutual Fund Marketing Fee*, or *12b-1 fee*. The Securities and Exchange Commission first approved this fee in 1980 to permit the mutual fund industry, which was in a slowdown at the time, to pass on to its customers the marketing costs, such as advertising and mailing costs, for the mutual fund. With a 12b-1 fee, you are, in effect, each year paying for the mutual fund to do more television and print advertising. Even though you are already invested in the fund, through the payment of this fee, you pay for the continual marketing of the fund to others. This cash cow varies from mutual fund to mutual fund with some, such as The Vanguard Group, charging fees of just a bit more than 4 percent of investor's profits while other mutual fund companies have marketing fees that take almost 16 percent of your profits. And what about the essential question as to why, year after year, you should as an investor have to pay for the marketing of the mutual fund company to other people.

With a 12b-1 fee, you are, in effect, each year paying for the mutual fund to do more television and print advertising.

So how do you compare the costs of different mutual funds to determine who is giving you the most bang for your buck and who has fees that might be considered by some to be a legal scam? An easy way to compare costs is to go to the Securities and Exchange Commission's Web site www.sec.gov and use its interactive Mutual Fund Cost Calculator to see how different funds compare.

TIP If you want to refine your investment choices to the simplest form, you may want to choose index funds. Index mutual funds are an investment arrangement by which a mutual fund holds all the securities in a particular index. Investment guru John Bogle of Vanguard Funds pioneered index funds. The particular index may be the S&P 500, the Wilshire 5000, or any of the many other index funds, some of which invest in the stocks of foreign countries, thereby facilitating your investing in emerging world markets. The theory of index funds is based on the fact that few people, if any, "beat" the market, particularly when you consider the additional costs of fees. Interestingly, over the past 15 years, index mutual funds have actually beaten actively managed funds by 3.4 percent. The expense costs for an actively managed no-load mutual fund may be six times that of an index fund.

TRUTH

57

Free financial seminars

Free financial seminars are common. Sometimes they are offered through mailings or advertisements in newspapers telling you about the investment seminar that will change your life. Sometimes they even provide a free lunch or at least coffee and doughnuts. But we all know there are no free lunches.

Sometimes the seminar you're invited to has a cost for tickets of as much as hundreds of dollars, but because you're "special," your invitation (along with just about everyone else's) has tickets to allow you to attend this costly seminar for free. At the seminar, you're told how to buy real estate with no money down, how to avoid income taxes, how to totally protect your assets from claims of all those people out there who are just waiting to sue you, or how to buy a unique investment that only they are offering that can earn you tremendous amounts of money in no time at all with no risk.

There are no free seminars.

The truth is, there are no free seminars. Even legitimate estate planning or investment seminars are not put on due to the goodness of the hearts of the seminar promoters. They're done to gather clients. They're done to sell you something. There are many legitimate "free" seminars, but scammers also put on free seminars, and they're adept at luring you into an investment, tax, or financial scheme that is nothing but a fraud.

Once again, do your homework. Check on the promoter of the seminar with the local Better Business Bureau, the Federal Trade Commission at www.ftc.gov, the Securities and Exchange Commission at www.sec.gov, and your state's Attorney General's office. Ignore any money-back guarantees that may be offered by the promoter of the seminar. If you don't know the promoter, how can you trust his guarantee? Be wary of the second step involved in many "free" seminars, which is the sale of books, CDs, software, videos, and other information to take you to the "profitable" level of their program. In these scams, this is just the beginning of the profitable level for the scammer, not for you. Beware of inflated promises. They tend to deflate quickly, as does your wallet.

TRUTH

Some solutions

t isn't that they can't see the solution.
It is that they can't see the problem.

—*G. K. Chesterton*

It's difficult to totally avoid being scammed or becoming a victim of identity theft. But there are some things that you can do to lessen your chances of becoming a victim. Some of these things are simple, while some require a little bit of work on your part. Many people are lazy and don't want to take these steps to protect their own security. These are the people that the scammers are counting on, because they're the easiest victims.

Do you really want to receive those unsolicited offers of credit cards and insurance that not only clutter your mailbox, but also provide ample opportunities for identity thieves to open credit in your name by either stealing your mail or stealing your trash if you merely throw out the solicitations without shredding them? And while we're on the subject, mere tearing of the solicitation or even straight shredding is not enough to protect you. Identity thieves often hire methamphetamine addicts with a predisposition to meticulous boring work to piece together your trash to provide a usable credit card offer.

You can avoid the entire problem by merely contacting the major credit reporting bureaus to have your name taken off the lists used to generate those offers. You can either call 888-567-8688 or go online at www.optoutprescreen.com to be removed from what the three credit reporting agencies—Experian, Equifax, and TransUnion—refer to as their prescreened offer lists. Your security will improve.

If you've been procrastinating taking yourself off the prescreened offer lists, a good time to act is when you apply for a mortgage. Once you apply for a mortgage, your name will be put on a "trigger list" maintained by the credit reporting bureaus that they sell to other mortgage lenders, and you'll soon be flooded with communications from other lenders. Of course, particularly after reading this book, you may be nervous about having your name removed from the prescreened offer lists, because when you call or go online to do so, you'll be asked for identifying information including your Social Security number. But the good news is that it's safe (or at least as safe as you can be) to give this information for the purpose of removing your name from these lists.

TRUTH

Keeping your computer secure

It seems that everyone does Windows, at least when it comes to a computer operating system. A key to avoiding fraud online is to keep your Windows software up-to-date with all the latest security updates. You'll be notified when new updates to your Windows operating system become available. Don't put off installing Windows security updates.

In addition to the updates of your Windows software, you should have a firewall and antivirus and antispyware software installed on your computer. Firewalls prevent outside computers from gaining access to your computer, although they're far from foolproof. However, like the lawyer joke about what do you call a hundred lawyers at the bottom of the sea: "It is a good start." There are many firewalls you can choose from. You can find out about free firewalls at www.free-firewall.org.

> Keep your Windows software up-to-date with all the latest security updates. You'll be notified when new updates to your Windows operating system become available.

Protect your computer with antivirus software such as Norton AntiVirus or McAfee VirusScan. Keep your subscription to whatever software you choose up-to-date. Your antivirus software is worthless unless it's constantly updated to prevent the latest attacks. Getting automatic updates is a good choice.

Install antispyware software such as Lavasoft's Ad-Aware, which can be found at www.adawareresource.com, or Spybot Search and Destroy 1.4, which can be found at www.safer-networking.org. Both of these are free, but once again be aware of proper spelling. There are phony versions of these programs that are spelled just slightly differently that are actually the very spyware that you're trying to avoid. Installing one of the phony software programs would only infect your computer rather than protect it. It sure is dangerous out there in cyberspace.

Some other choices include Zone Labs' Zone Alarm Internet Security Suite, which combines antivirus, antispyware, and antispam protection.

Some good antispyware that is not free, but reasonably priced and worth the money, include F-Secure's Anti-Spyware and Lavasoft's Ad-Aware SW Plus 1.06.

TIP Scammers gain access to your computer to implant keystroke logging programs and other malware. Downloading "free" computer games, screensavers, or music is a quick way to compromise your computer, affect your security, and increase your susceptibility to identity theft. Even downloading what you may think are free software programs to protect your computer from hackers may jeopardize you because you may be downloading the very malware you're trying to avoid. Always be sure of the source of anything that you download online.

Zombies

Anyone who ever saw the *Night of the Living Dead* movies, particularly the first one, knows that zombies are pretty scary creatures. But as scary as they are, chances are pretty good that you'll not be attacked by one of those kinds of zombies. However, the chances of your being attacked over the Internet and having your computer turned into a zombie computer is a very real threat to anyone who goes online.

Scammers who want to avoid detection send out viruses to the computers of unwary victims that turn their computers into zombies. Through your computer and those of other victims, a network is formed known as a *botnet*. The scammer then can use your computer to send out malware that may take the form of spam, Trojan horse keystroke logging programs, or even major denial-of-service attacks. *Denial-of-service attacks* occur when your computer and other zombies in the botnet

> The chances of your being attacked over the Internet and having your computer turned into a zombie computer is a very real threat to anyone who goes online.

flood a target Web site with data requests that it can't handle. The targeted Web site is effectively shut down as a result of such an attack. Threats of denial-of-service attacks have been used to extort money from major online businesses. At one time, it took some significant computer skills to create a zombie virus botnet, but now the technology has been dumbed down and sells for as little as $20 to criminals looking for a new opportunity to scam the public.

Sometimes it's difficult to know that your computer has been turned into a zombie. Some possible clues may be difficulty sending emails or using the Internet or blood seeping out of the keyboard. Okay, I was just kidding about the blood and the keyboard. You may even notice emails that are returned to you as being undelivered that you didn't send. If you have any concern that your computer is a zombie, have your computer scanned thoroughly by an expert to learn if it has been turned into part of a botnet and to remove the infection.

- **Security patches**—The proverbial ounce of prevention is worth a pound of cure has never been more accurate than in dealing with an infected computer that has been turned into a zombie. It is much easier to prevent the problem than to clean up the mess after the fact. Prowling cyberspace are worms looking for computers that have security flaws and holes to exploit. Windows software is the most commonly used computer operating system. Like all systems, it has flaws. Microsoft does a good job of constantly updating its system with security patches, and it notifies people to install these security patches. Far too many people don't. Don't be one of those people. Update your software with security patches as soon as you're notified.

- **Unsolicited emails and downloads**—Most malware, spyware, and zombie viruses attack your computer through unsolicited emails. Don't open any email if you're at all uncomfortable with it. And never download attachments from someone whom you're not totally confident is legitimate. It's in these attachments that many of these viruses come in. Also, many viruses and other malware come from sharing files with people you're not familiar with. Sharing music or games is a risky business even with people you know, because you don't know where their computer has been. They may be passing on not just their music but also an infection.

- **Change your browser**—You may even want to indulge in a little overkill protection by considering using a browser other than Internet Explorer, which is, at the moment, the browser of choice of scammers sending zombie viruses. Alternative browsers such as Firefox are a good choice.

TRUTH

Wi-Fi

Free Wi-Fi hot spots are computer networks made available as a free accommodation by restaurants, coffee shops, malls, and airports; however, rarely are they very secure.

And even if a legitimate Wi-Fi hot spot were secure, you would still run the danger of using a Wi-Fi hot spot that is operated by an identity thief through a peer-to-peer network set up by a nearby computer hacker who is plugged into the Internet. This hacker's network permits you to connect to the Internet through his connection rather than independently connecting to the Internet on your own. Because you're connected to the hacker's laptop, he sees everything you do online and may even be able to access your files through file sharing. He also is now able to install a Trojan horse keystroke logging program on your computer without your being aware of it.

So what can you do to protect yourself? To avoid the hacker and phony Wi-Fi connection, you should disconnect your computer's ad hoc mode, which enables your computer to connect without wires to another computer, before you use Wi-Fi. You should also turn off your file-sharing capabilities before using a Wi-Fi hot spot.

If you use the new Microsoft Vista operating system, you should turn off the Network Discovery feature that alerts other network users of your availability for connection. You should also use software that encrypts your email so that anyone who is able to intercept it will be unable to read it.

Use a USB flash drive to hold the programs you need and your personal data in an encrypted form.

It's a good policy not to keep any sensitive private data on the hard drive of your laptop. Judging by the many stories of laptops full of unencrypted, sensitive information being stolen, this policy is not being followed enough by many people in business and government. Use a USB flash drive to hold the programs you need and your personal data in an encrypted form. When you boot up at a Wi-Fi hotspot, use the USB drive so that even if someone were able to get through your firewall and other security programs, he would be unable to obtain any useable information from your laptop computer.

TRUTH

61

Due diligence

Before investing in anything, you should always do your homework.

To assist in evaluating the broker or salesman looking to sell you an investment, go to the BrokerCheck service of the National Association of Securities Dealers (NASD), a private regulatory organization at www.nasd.com/index.htm, or call them at 800-289-9999 to confirm that the salesperson is licensed to sell investments. You can also check at that Web site to learn whether there are any complaints against the broker as well as any disciplinary proceedings or criminal convictions. In addition, you can check on whether the investment itself is registered. Follow this up with a look into these same issues with your own state securities regulators and the Securities and Exchange Commission (SEC).

For business opportunities, contact the Better Business Bureau to see if there are any relevant complaints by going to its Web site at www.bbb.org. Also check with the Federal Trade Commission at www.ftc.gov and the consumer protection division of your state's Attorney General.

Finally, when in doubt—and you should always have a little doubt—do what you always do when you need some information. Google it. Check out the investment and particularly the person pitching it to you on Google and other search engines. Don't forget to try a search with the salesman's name and the word *scam*. It might save you some money.

Some final words

Knowledge is the key to making ourselves safe from scams— knowledge of ourselves and our own weaknesses as well as knowledge of the dangers that lurk in so many places.

> Knowledge is the key to making ourselves safe from scams.

Some people are overwhelmed by a fear of being scammed, but this kind of paralyzing fear serves no useful purpose. It's better to heed the words of James Thurber, who said, "Let us not look back in anger or forward in fear, but around in awareness." Be aware, and you'll be all right.

Acknowledgments

Writing is a very solitary exercise, yet it cannot be done without the help and support of so many people. I want to thank the following people who have helped me so much, often without even knowing of the assistance they provided.

Russ Hall and Jim Boyd of Prentice Hall, who helped mold my ramblings.

Ron Nathan and Karen Muller, who year after year open their home in Florida for me and provide me with a place to write.

Fran Borek and Gerry Smith, whose hospitality in Stowe, Vermont, makes it impossible not to write.

Carol Hepburn, who keeps me informed.

Steve Lichtenstein and the administration of Bentley College for their encouragement and support.

Marc Padellaro, as good a friend as he is a lawyer, and he is as good a lawyer as there is.

Tom Freda, who keeps me from being complacent in my thinking. He makes me think.

Jim Brick, a supportive friend and colleague.

Joe "The Pro" Monahan, who knows how to tell a story.

Tony Pelusi, a lawyer who has found so much more than the law.

Michael Harrison, a friend, mentor, and partner who has helped guide my career.

Saul Chadis, Peter Ettenberg, Marty Kenney, Bruce Newman, and Peter Seronick—old friendships never grow old.

My parents, Jeanne and Arnie Weisman, who continue to teach me more than I could ever tell.

About the Author

Steve Weisman hosts the nationally syndicated radio show "A Touch of Grey," heard on more than 50 stations, including WABC in New York City and KRLA in Los Angeles. He is a practicing lawyer and is admitted to practice before the United States Supreme Court. He is a sought-after public speaker and commentator and has appeared on many radio and television shows throughout the country. He is the Legal Editor of *Talkers Magazine*, the preeminent trade publication of talk radio. Along with being a practicing attorney, Steve is a Senior Lecturer at Bentley College in Waltham, Massachusetts. His books include *A Guide to Elder Planning*, *50 Ways to Protect Your Identity and Your Credit*, and *Boomer or Bust*, all published by Pearson.

Simply the best thinking

THE TRUTH AND NOTHING BUT THE TRUTH

The **Truth About** Series offers the collected and distilled knowledge on a topic and shows you how you to apply this knowledge in your everyday life.

Life is a negotiation. Negotiation is an elemental part of one's professional life. Learn why great negotiators are taught and not born.

ISBN: 0136007368
Leigh Thompson
$18.99

Learn real solutions for the tough challenges faced by every business leader who needs to drive and sustain successful change.

ISBN: 0132354624
William Kane
$18.99

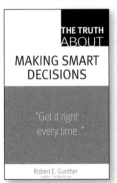

Get the right information, act decisively, and give yourself the best chance for success.

ISBN: 0132354632
Robert E. Gunther
$18.99

Also Available

The Truth About Confident Presenting
The Truth About Managing People
The Truth About Getting the Best from People